Knapp

D1712074

CONCEPTS AND CASES IN FASHION BUYING AND MERCHANDISING

Sidney Packard

Associate Professor:
Fashion Buying and
Merchandising
Department of the
Fashion Institute of
Technology

Nathan Axelrod

Former Professor and Chairman:
Fashion Buying and
Merchandising
Department of the
Fashion Institute of
Technology

Fairchild Publications
New York

PREFACE

Fashion merchandising is essentially an art, one that requires, like any art form, a hands-on-experience. The excitement, the decision making, and the manifold relationships are fully realized in daily business encounters.

Concepts and Cases in Fashion Buying and Merchandising was conceived to serve the following purposes:

1. To enable the reader to apply and to reinforce the material discussed in *Fashion Buying and Merchandising.**
2. To free students from the task of taking notes. *Fashion Buying and Merchandising* was designed to eliminate, to the greatest degree, the lecturing need by the instructor; this text therefore completes the restraints of structured classroom sessions. A seminar-like atmosphere should be possible with give-and-take based on free expression. This teaching method can be a stimulating, action-based program that should develop a variety of interpretations of many merchandising principles.
3. To train and develop case method thinking so that students realize that:
   A. There is never any one "solution" to a problem.
   B. Data must be available to support a position — pro or con.
   C. Selected alternatives are not solutions.
   D. Logic is not necessarily truth.
   E. Executives must accept responsibility for decisions based on logical reasons.

The concepts that precede each section are brief summaries of the fundamentals of buying and merchandising. The intention is merely to afford a review of the basics before attempting to "solve" the problems. In these explanation, efforts were made to use the vocabulary, practices, relationships, and practical applications.

Following each section, related case problems are narrated which do not include all possible details. This is a normal situation because in the business world many details are frequently lacking, too.

Sidney Packard
New York, New York

Nathan Axelrod
Hallandale, Florida

---

* Sidney Packard, Arthur A. Winters, and Nathan Axelrod, *Fashion Buying and Merchandising* (New York: Fairchild Publications, 1976).

TABLE OF CONTENTS

I   The Case Study Method 1

II The Meaning and Implications of Fashion
    Merchandising 17
    1. The Men's Wear Buyer's Frustration 26
    2. Customer Segmentation Importance 29
    3. The Impossible Goals 31

III Fashion Buying as a Career 33
    4. Terri's Tearful Tale 36
    5. The Executive Trainee 38

IV Common Knowledge for Fashion Buyers 41
    6. Tying One On 46
    7. The Cashmere Sweater 48
    8. The New Lingerie Buyer 51

V   The Organization of a Large Retail Store 53
    9. Stockwork: The Buyer's Bane 61
    10. Is the Customer Always Right? 63
    11. The Old Guard Never Retreats 65
    12. The General Merchandise Manager has a Problem   67

VI The Fashion Buyer's Responsibilities in a Large Retail
    Store 71
    13. The Price Change 77
    14. Restraint of Trade? 79
    15. A Retail Tug of War 81
    16. The Power of the Pencil 84

VII Fashion Buying for Central Chain and Mail-Order
    Organizations 87
    17. Sam, You Made the Pants Too Short 92
    18. The Improvident Cancellation 94
    19. Pity the Poor Manager 97

VIII The Resident Buying Office 101
    20. Should All the Eggs Go in One Basket? 109
    21. Ethics 111
    22. The Catalogue 112

IX   Fashion Buying for the Small Independent Store 115
    23. The Small Store Dilemma 119
    24. An Overstocked Condition.. 121
    25. The Entrepreneurs 123

X   Assisting the Buyer or Steps Leading to the Position of
    Buyer 125
    26. Branch Store Problem... 133
    27. Big Fish in a Little Pond. 135
    28. The Coverup.. 138
    29. Sell! Sell! Sell! 140

XI   Dollar Planning and Control—Quantitative Planning.... 143
    30. The Planning Impasse... 150
    31. A Fur Story 152
    32. Shooting Craps 153
    33. The Inexperienced Buyer.. 155

XII   Merchandise Assortment Planning—Qualitative
    Planning 157
    34. To Brand or Not To Brand 164
    35. You Can't Win Them All 166
    36. Who are the Customers? 168

XIII   Selection of Resources 171
    37. You're Only Young Once.. 178
    38. When It Rains, It Pours 180
    39. The Merchandise by Any Other Label 182

XIV   Fashion Buying Practices and Techniques....................... 185
    40. Buying Ethics 194
    41. Inventory Maneuvers 197
    42. The "Knock Off" 199
    43. Buying Practices... 201
    44. The Off-Price Promotion 203
    45. Mort Heller Made a Big Boo-Boo.............................. 206

XV   Sales Promotion.. 209
    46. The Founder's Day Special 217
    47. Does No Mean Never 219
    48. Double Trouble 221

THE CASE STUDY METHOD

DEFINITION

What is the *case study method?*

First, one may ask the question: "What is a *case?*"

A case is a description of a real situation.[1] A case typically is a record of a business issue which actually has been faced by a business executive, together with surrounding facts, opinions, and prejudices upon which executive decisions had to depend.[2] A case raises issues and provides material with which to analyze or deal with these issues. It is an account of a real situation in which issues need to be recognized and dealt with in some meaningful way.[3]

Here, then, is a multi-faceted answer to our question—a case describes a realistic situation or problem. It is not to be confused with an incident or an illustration which some business educators are now using and calling "a mini-case" (not that a case is required to be long or short in size or duration). As long as the case gives the student *sufficient* information—not necessarily *complete* information, since business frequently does not have all the facts—the student may be expected to be able to deal with the case.

The important point about the case is that the events described actually happened and the student is asked to examine a real

---

1. Raymond Simson, *Distribution by the Case.* London: Distributive Trades Education and Training Council, 1973, p. 9.
2. Malcolm P. McNair, Elizabeth A. Burnham, and Anita C. Hersum, *Cases in Retail Management.* New York: McGraw-Hill, Inc., 1957, p. vii.
3. Melvin J. Stranford, "Every Teacher a Case Writer," *Collegiate News and Views,* Spring, 1974, p. 9.

situation. This distinguishes the case method from the business game or the business exercise—the strength of the case method lies in this *reality*. However the participants may disagree with the actions taken by management et al during or following the incident described, the starting point for all discussion is the hard fact that this is a real, not an imaginary situation.[4]

These "real" cases are either written in narrative form by the instructor or assigned to the student from the many case books (such as this one) available in various subject areas. In the use of the case method, the student is given sufficient material which will enable him to *think* about the problem(s) raised in each case. It is this reliance on *thinking* that the case method differs from the other educational processes such as lecturing, memorizing, testing for skill development.

Professor Charles I. Gragg, long a pioneer in the use of the case method at The Harvard Business School, wrote almost four decades ago: "It can be said flatly that the mere act of listening to wise statements and sound advice does little for anyone. In the process of learning, the learners dynamic cooperation is required. Such cooperation from students does not arise automatically, however. It has to be provided for and continually encouraged . . . By opening the way for students to make positive contributions to thought . . . and thus prepare themselves for action."[5]

HISTORY AND DEVELOPMENT

It is generally assumed that the case method originated at Harvard University about a century ago and was first used at The Harvard Law School as a means of helping students to think for themselves. The Harvard Graduate School of Business as a center for developing administrative ability decided early in its career to stress, not only independent thinking, but also to develop in the students the ability to slash through all sorts of tangled and intertwined facts, events, incidents, personalities, etc. The faculty insisted that the graduate student learn to distinguish principles, policies or ideas that have general applicability as well as long-term validity. Accordingly, the case study method is used there to this day.

Another interesting aspect of the development of the case study method at Harvard was the role of the instructor. He was seen

---

4. Stranford, "Every Teacher a Case Writer," p. 9.
5. Charles I. Gragg, "Because Wisdom Can't Be Told," *Harvard Alumni Bulletin*, October 19, 1940.

not as a lecturer, but as a catalytic agent who assigned cases for study and analysis, and then continually provided the proper environment for group discussion in his classroom. He never "tells" (lectures) but he acts as a "guide" during the learning process. He tries to help the student discover the ideas contained in the facts provided by the case reports.

There are a number of other methods of teaching with case studies which have been developed by other centers of higher education. For example, the Wharton School of Business of the University of Pennsylvania has its "live case" method; the British Administration Staff College at Henley, England, has developed the "syndicate method"; and the Massachusetts Institute of Technology uses the "incident process." While the approaches of these and other forms of the case method seem to differ, essentially they are attempting to do the same thing—to involve the student in thinking and analyzing, individually and collectively.[6]

ADVANTAGES OF THE CASE STUDY METHOD

There are many benefits to the student from the use of the case method in the classroom:

1. The case method brings an aspect of *reality* to the learning process that is missing from so much of business education. It is a departure from theory and it focuses the business student's attention on the *realism* of the business world where decisions have to be made constantly.
2. The case method encourages and even demands that the student rely on his own *thinking* and his ability to develop the power of *analyzing* that is required by those who hold or who aspire to some level of managerial responsibility. This is particularly true because while there may be some similarity between cases, most cases differ from each other in one or more details. Thus, the issues and selected alternatives will be different.
3. The case method helps the student to develop sound *judgment* in making decisions that are required of managers. While it is true that the case method is *learning by doing*, it is not a substitute for actual business experience. But it

6. Nathan Axelrod, "Teaching by the Case Method" (Paper delivered before the Annual Meeting of the New York State Association of Junior Colleges, New York, 1969).

is certainly one of the better types of preparation for making that (business) experience fruitful.[7]

4. The case method helps to develop the ability to both write and speak more fluently and clearly. The reader will discover in Chapter III of this text the need for those who desire to succeed in the field of fashion buying and merchandising to have both the power to express themselves orally as well as to be able to write well. (In another section of this discussion of the case method, the reader will also become aware of the oral and written aspects of a regular case study session or group.)

5. This ability to communicate which is required by the case method, "student participation is achieved by the opening of *free* channels of communication between students and students; and between students and instructors ... the confidence the student can be given ... that he can and is expected to make contributions to the understanding of the group, is a powerful encouragement to effort."[8]

6. The case method is based on the educational philosophy of learning by doing. This means that both the case itself and the instructor must put the students into a psychological frame of mind of believing that they are the supervisors or the managers. This is helpful in not only developing the ability to think analytically, but also to develop the ability to make decisions by probing for issues or policies or principles, weighing alternatives, and then hopefully arriving at a possible alternative that will prove to be effective when put into use.

7. The case method is *enjoyed* by "mature" students with suitable academic pre-requisites (upperclass and postgraduate students, industry executives, or trainees with adequate college preparation) because:

   A. They are free from lectures, exercises, tests, etc.; probably for the first time in their academic careers.

   B. They are being treated as professionals and they like that feeling.

   C. They are all in the same boat. Everyone in the group or class has the need to give as well as to receive ideas based on their own thinking. This is genuine intercom-

---

7. L.C. Lockley, Charles J. Dirksen, and A. Kroeger, *Cases in Marketing,* Fourth Edition. Boston: Allyn and Bacon, Inc., 1971, p. 2.
8. Charles I. Gragg, "Because Wisdom Can't Be Told."

munication, a rarity in the average learning situation.
  D. They like the idea of being in a class or group where, strictly speaking (as we shall see later in this section), there are no *right* or *wrong* answers; and where there is rarely only one alternative to the problem.
  E. They like the feeling of being in management's shoes, making decisions, etc. The case method brings students closer to visualizing their goals for future job prospects. Thus, when a student analyzes a case in fashion merchandising, he or she simulates what must be done by the buyer or the merchandise manager. This gives the student the opportunity to gain "experience" by applying general knowledge from all other merchandising courses and work experience.

DISADVANTAGES OF THE CASE STUDY METHOD

The case method has some shortcomings and should not be thought of as "be all and end all" of business education or management training. Among the disadvantages that are immediately obvious:

1. The case method is not readily usable by all students. It is most suitable for advanced students or experienced personnel who have a heavy background in their major area in addition to the maturity which comes from a number of years of previous academic study or business experience.
2. The case method, when used in industry, has a similar disadvantage when it is used for training junior executives. Like the upperclass students referred to in #1 above, the lack of practical executive experience will soon become apparent.
3. The case method's provision for students to participate in simulated management decision making is not a true situation. The student too easily feels the synthetic nature of this role playing. He feels that in actuality there is no real responsibility or authority to do what needs to be done.
4. The case method's severest critics feel that even actual role playing is not a substitute for those ingredients that are missing from real life situations such as pressure, time factors, competition, antagonisms, prejudices, background noises and other pollutants.

5. The case method is also criticized because of the cases themselves. These anti-case study critics claim, with some measure of correctness, that many cases are products of oversimplification, that they tend to be too orderly and too compact.

6. The case method may be confusing to the reader who frequently feels that there are not enough facts or information presented in the case to arrive at a sound decision. This is a normal situation, even in business, because the executive is frequently faced with a problem without all the facts he would like to have because there has not been time to get them.[9]

7. The case method is difficult to "sell" to *instructors* because:

   A. It is a "new" method for them—they feel unsure or insecure about leaving the lecture-recitation pattern.

   B. It appears to them to place too much emphasis on the role of the student and to put them in a lesser light—not likely to please many instructors who are accustomed to being "on stage, center."

   C. It seems to them that the case method takes too much time in class. They (and sometimes students) believe that this will decrease the amount of time available "to cover all the work."

   D. They believe that the case method is only good for "superior" or "better" students and that the "average" student will quickly get lost in the morass of problem solving or decision making that is quite beyond his ability.

   E. The administrator that is not too familiar with the case method may look askance at the instructor's role (described later in this section); they may tend to view it with alarm as an opportunity for the instructor to "goof off," to rest up after a hard night, to stall for time, etc.

It should be apparent from this book that your authors believe that not only do the advantages outweigh the disadvantages by far, but that some of the disadvantages or criticisms leveled are specious and without merit. While we do not believe that the

---

9. Nathan Axelrod, *Selected Cases in Fashion Marketing*. New York: ITT Educational Services, 1968. Vol. I, p. 2.

case method is the solution to all of business education's teaching problems, we do feel that it is a well established, participative learning process. This is not to put down the lecture-recitation method or book-reliance methods of gaining large measures of knowledge—each has its place and they should be used to supplement and complement each other.

CASE STUDY METHODOLOGY

It should be made clear at the outset that there is no single, preferred or ordained procedure for conducting the case method. However, your authors are offering the following information in order to assist both the instructor and the student:

- The role of the student in the case study method
- The role of the instructor in the case study method
- A suggested check list for analyzing a case
- A sample form for case method analysis reporting
- A sample case "Classification by Confusion"
- A step-by-step solution of the sample case (using the sample form)

THE ROLE OF THE STUDENT IN THE CASE STUDY METHOD

It has been said that the case method is a student-dominated method of learning. This has been intended as an unfavorable criticism, but educators and management trainers believe that a student-dominated situation is an advantage rather than a limitation.

The following are some considerations for the student's attention:

1. At the outset, the student will find the case method confusing because he has not yet built up a knowledge of conditions and procedures of the subject area. Also, the student is probably not used to informal problem solving.[10]
2. The student will find the role of the case method class instructor to be somewhat different from his past learning experiences. The instructor will be there to raise pointed questions, to challenge the individual's as well as the group's thinking, and to encourage discussion. The in-

---

10. L.C. Lockley and Charles J. Dirksen, *Cases in Marketing*, Third Edition. Boston: Allyn and Bacon, Inc., 1964, p. 11.

structor will be present at all times, of course, but he will
be a guide rather than a lecturer.[11]

3. Like the merchandising/managerial position to which he
   aspires, the student may find in the case method that he
   does not have sufficient data to solve the problem cor-
   rectly. The student is herewith assured that this is par for
   the course—a normal situation. Executives learn early in
   their careers that they do not have all the knowledge they
   need for any given circumstances, that they will have to
   make do with what they know, and make suppositions or
   presumptions based on available data.

4. The student or other case method participants will soon
   learn that there is no room for "the back-seater." Unlike
   the other traditional teaching methods, this requires active, heavy participation on the part of each member of
   the group.

   In addition, the student will also become cognizant of
   the value and worth of the others in the group as well as
   the need for dealing with the opinions or contributions of
   these associates to the group as a whole.

5. If the instructor uses the student-chairperson approach to
   conduct case method sessions, those who accept such a
   position will benefit greatly in terms of developing skills
   in conducting all types of discussion groups. The self-confi-
   dence that will accrue from such experiences will not only
   benefit the students directly, but will also give them experience in their later supervisory lives.

THE ROLE OF THE INSTRUCTOR IN THE CASE STUDY METHOD

As indicated previously, the instructor who uses the case study
method does not act as a teacher (other than instructing the students
early in the course in the use of the case method). The instructor
"guides," where necessary, to reach a conclusion that satisfies the
needs of the group.

In addition, the instructor has the following tasks:

1. To assign specific cases to the group and to require that
   the members:
   A. Read those cases thoroughly.

---

11. Axelrod, *Selected Cases in Fashion Marketing*, Vol. I, p. 3.

    B. Study the material therein.

    C. Secure *outside* information such as text or reference books on marketing or merchandising, trade papers, magazines.

    D. Do personal observation and research in the field.

    E. Draw on past experience as a consumer and employee.

2. To appoint student discussion leaders after training the entire class in the duties of a case method session chairperson.

3. To decide which form of the case method technique is best suited for that specific occasion. The instructor may use:

    A. The regular, structured, *narrative* form such as found in this book. Inferred in the use of this technique is the question of what the group would or should do in each specific case.

    B. Role playing, a technique utilizing the dramatization of a problem by carefully chosen "players." These are members of the group who use the facts given in the case to enact the situation as they interpret it. The entire group becomes involved by identifying with the players.

    C. The *buzz* group or *committee* system, involves dividing the group into equal (and hopefully homogeneous) groups of students. Each group works on the case study separately for a given amount of time. Then, a group-chosen "reporter" gives his group's analysis of the case. Similarities in the committee reports are merely noted; differences of opinion are discussed by the entire group.

    D. *Brain-storming* is a group technique whereby the members are given a topic on some phase of merchandising or management. The members of the group, under the leader's guidance, are encouraged to throw out all sorts of suggestions without giving thought to such matters as cost or practicality. Members of the group are also encouraged to "piggyback" on other's suggestions. The use of negativism in either suggestions or objections is strictly forbidden.

      It should be noted that the use of the *narrative* or *descriptive* case study technique is one that will be most frequently or commonly used. However, the other techniques described above, particularly the committee system, may be used from time to time to provide variety.

4. While the student tends to enjoy the case method as opposed to the traditional forms of learning, the instructor must be able not only to measure the student's contribution to the group's actions, but must also be able to determine by means of written tests and original case writing assignments how well the student understands the case method.

5. It cannot be emphasized too emphatically that the case method instructor is not teaching by the traditional method. He must be aware of his duties as a "guide." Even if there is a student leader for each case, the instructor should:

    A. Interject his ideas where needed.
    B. Act as a judge of the facts.
    C. Keep the case moving along smoothly; especially where there appears to be something stalling it—get it off dead center.
    D. Act as the "devil's advocate" to provide motivation that may be needed from time to time.
    E. Encourage the group when answers are not easily forthcoming.

6. Obviously, the instructor must be well prepared. He must not only know every phase of the case thoroughly (by having read and re-read it) but he must do his homework by completely analyzing the case itself well in advance. As the patient will have little confidence in his doctor when he sees hesitation in the conduct of his case, so the group will lose interest if the instructor is uncertain about any aspect of their case.

A SUGGESTED CHECK LIST FOR ANALYZING A CASE

There are many ways, techniques or variations available in the procedure of the case study method. Your authors, however, would be derelict in their duty if they did not recommend at least one standard method of handling a case study.

1. Read and re-read the case narrative until you are completely familiar with the facts involved.

2. Determine the *immediate* problem—what was it that caused the case to come into existence—if *this* had not

occurred, there actually would not have been a case.

3. Most importantly—the only reason for studying this or any case—what are the *central* or *basic issues* involved. What fundamental principles or policies or generalizations may be determined.

4. What are the practical, non-academic, *alternative solutions* to the problem presented in the case? Are each of these solutions practical for use in the business world? Why? If not, why not.

5. What is the best alternative? Why? Will it work under normal business conditions?

6. After analyzing the case in your mind (as indicated in 1–5 above), write up the case in a manner desired by the instructor (a suggested sample form follows).

7. Be sure to make a duplicate copy of the case report for class use. Bring to class your notes or any outside data that may be available.

A SAMPLE FORM FOR CASE METHOD ANALYSIS REPORTING

The following is a suggested form which the student may use to assist in class participation as well as to submit to the instructor at the start of the class as evidence of prior preparation. Some instructors may have this form duplicated and distributed to students as is or modified to suit the group's purposes.

1. *Immediate Problem*

2. *Central Issue(s)*

3. *Alternatives*

Space should be allotted for at least two, or for as many as four or five, alternatives.

Students should be required to both defend and to admit weaknesses or limitations of each alternative.

4. *Selected Alternatives*

Select the best of the alternatives. Students should be asked to justify the reason(s) for making this choice.

A SAMPLE CASE "CLASSIFICATION BY CONFUSION"

In this section, we present a sample case, entitled, "Classification by Confusion," in the field of fashion merchandising and in the following section, a sample case analysis report "solving" this case.

Classification by Confusion

Chase Department Store, which has an annual sales volume of $12 million, is located in a fairly large mid-southeastern city of the United States. The climate generally ranges from mild to hot almost all year-round and while there may be some cold days during the fall and winter months, the annual temperature range is about seventy degrees. This weather is ideal for the tennis craze that is sweeping the country and that is making this sport the number one activity among the "in crowd."

In addition, while the area is predominantly agricultural in nature, big industries such as textiles, paper, chemicals are gradually making themselves felt more and more in the area's economy. These industrial giants bring a younger, more affluent group of customers to Chase's and have required the store's management to "think fashion" somewhat differently than their competitors because Chase has always been known as "the better store in town." All in all, the influx of a younger, professional population and their families has been good for the store.

Elizabeth Howe has been the sportswear buyer for Chase for the past three years, having come from a large midwestern metropolis where she had been an associate buyer of active sportswear. She is very happy at the store, is doing a good job, and is well thought of by the management.

On her annual trip to the Los Angeles sportswear market, Howe bought something new for Chase—a white tennis dress for those who did not play tennis—a sort of après-tennis outfit. When the merchandise arrived, it was ticketed, and she had her assistant arrange a good-size sample assortment on a T-stand at the entrance to the department.

As it happened, this location coincided with the western perimeter of the Junior Dress Department. Sandra McMillan, the junior dress buyer, practically fell over this new merchandise and almost immediately strode into Elizabeth Howe's office, which was back to back with hers.

"Hey, Liz, where do you come off selling white dresses in your Sportswear Department, and flaunting them under my nose at that."

"If you look closely, they are not really dresses. They are tennis outfits as their labels plainly state," replied Howe. "I bought them from Miss California, my biggest Los Angeles sportswear resource."

McMillan persisted. "And another thing, it's not bad enough that you're carrying them right next to my department but they're priced $3 less than similar ones that I'm loaded with in my own stock."

"Sandy, you know that the sportswear market prices are generally lower than dress prices," answered Liz. "You know they have a different labor setup and that sportswear workmanship is not tailored as well as dresses. And anyway, Sandy, you remember when you brought in that big line of pantsuits from Capital Dresses, that were definitely sportswear items, I went along with it although I knew that you would hurt my business, but since they were from one of your regular dress resources. . . ."

But Sandra McMillan was not to be mollified. She saw these tennis dresses as a potential threat to her department, especially in view of the snowballing tennis hobby.

Accordingly, she sought J. Laurence Bennett, the ready-to-wear merchandise manager and discussed the full impact of her gripe against Howe's action. Bennett listened carefully and promised to check into the matter at once.

He called Howe into his office and got her side of the story, including her reasons for making the purchase.

Bennett is relatively new to Chase, having come from New York City where he had been a dress buyer for a famous Fifth Avenue store. He is generally regarded as an astute merchandiser and he is not known to play favorites among the buyers under his supervision.

If you were in J. Laurence Bennett's place, what would you do?

A STEP-BY-STEP SOLUTION OF THE SAMPLE CASE
(using the sample form)

1. *Immediate Problem*
   The dress buyer discovers that the neighboring Sportswear Department is selling a similar (tennis) dress at a lower price.
2. *Central Issue(s)*
   A basic merchandising principle: A merchandise classification belongs to the store, not to any individual buyer.
3. *Alternatives*
   A. Leave the situation as it is now—status quo.
      (1) Advantages
         (a) It is the easy way out—let it be.

(b) A buyer should be able to use her own resources.

(2) Disadvantages

(a) Unfair competition for the Dress Department.

(b) Customer confusion may arise as to price and merchandise location.

B. Transfer the merchandise to the Sportswear Department from the Dress Department by a bookkeeping transaction, after the Dress Department takes a markdown of $3 to bring the merchandise in line with the Sportswear Department's price.

(1) Advantages

(a) It is an easy, simple solution.

(b) Customers get the best buys, building good customer relations. No more confusion because only one department is selling the item.

(2) Disadvantages

(a) Dresses belong in a Dress Department—axiomatic.

(b) Customers generally look for dresses in a Dress Department.

(c) Better quality in dress market than in sportswear—important to maintain quality standards.

C. Transfer the merchandise from the Sportswear Department to the Dress Department by a bookkeeping transaction with the Dress Department taking a markup of $3 to bring the merchandise in line with the Dress Department's price.

(1) Advantages

(a) It is an easy, simple solution.

(b) Customers will not be confused because the merchandise will be selling in one department only.

(c) Dresses belong in a Dress Department.

(2) Disadvantages

(a) Customers are not getting the best possible price.

(b) It is a sportswear item and should be sold there.

D. Take the merchandise from both the Dress and Sportswear Departments and sell in the Sporting Goods Department.

(1) Advantages
    (a) A natural place for such outfits to be sold.
    (b) It is a neutral ground and avoids conflict be-
        tween the clothing buyers.

(2) Disadvantages
    (a) The sporting goods buyer is not qualified to
        buy such fashion merchandise.
    (b) The salespeople in the Sporting Goods Depart-
        ment are equally untrained.
    (c) The Sporting Goods Department does not
        have adequate facilities such as Dressing
        Rooms for the sale of such merchandise.

4. *Selected Alternatives*
Leave the situation as it is now—status quo.

A. These are the days of "scrambled merchandising" and customers are accustomed to competition within stores.

B. A buyer usually has the right to buy the offerings of what manufacturers consider a trend of their market.

C. Precedent (knitted dresses, pantsuits, golf dresses, knitted suits, two-piece dresses, etc.) favors the maintenance of stock in both the Sportswear and Dress Departments.

II

THE MEANING AND IMPLICATIONS OF FASHION MERCHANDISING

DEFINITION

The word fashion, like many English words, has many meanings. As a part of speech it can be used both as a noun and a verb. As a noun, it can denote make, form, shape, kind, sort, manner, speech, conduct. As a verb, the dictionary lists the following uses: make, contrive, form, fit, shape. Since there is a variety of correct meanings, it is necessary to establish the connotative meaning, the interpretation of the word within the context of our study—what we are saying when we use it.

For our study, fashion is apparel that is accepted by a substantial group of people at a given time, in a given place. Hence, there are four elements: *people, acceptance, time,* and *place.*

A common mistake is to equate the word substantial with majority. Just imagine if the standard were the acceptance by a majority. We would be virtually wearing uniforms. This could be the case in some countries where the economy is run by political command, but hardly the case in the United States where there is a myriad of choice and sufficient per capita income for individuals to express some individuality. So, it is rare for majority acceptance. Such rarity did occur among the young with the acceptance of blue jeans, the most universal fashion of all time.

How many is *substantial* is relative, and really dependent upon the type of fashion. High fashion could refer to a group of two hundred wealthy people who have embraced a dress costing $1,000. Therefore we have high fashion, those accepted by a limited number of people. On the other side of the coin, one thousand students could decorate their jeans with decals of popular slogans.

Fashion can be regional, sub-cultural, national, and international. Fashions are also related to time, some are short-lived and referred to as *fads;* some are long lasting and referred to as *classics;* and some are inherent to the society (handed down from generation to generation) and become part of the culture.

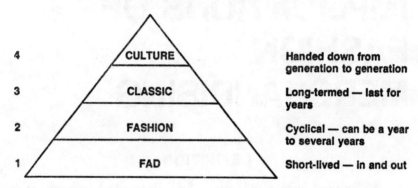

FIGURE 1 A SCALE OF COMPARATIVE TIME VALUES OF FASHION

Examples for each group:

1. Nehru suit
2. Shorter length hemlines
3. Shirtwaist dress
4. Blue Jeans

THE EVOLUTIONARY CHARACTER OF FASHION

Although we tend to believe that fashion bursts on the scene, it is not the case; it is almost an imperceptible process. There is a period of gradual acceptance during which the elements of the new idea grows on us—with more people relating to it with the passage of time. As one wag once said, fashion is something we find ludicrous, laugh at, smile at, and finally fight to retain. Psychologically, the acceptance of the new requires the discarding of the old. The relegating of usable clothing to the "give away pile" is also an economic cost.

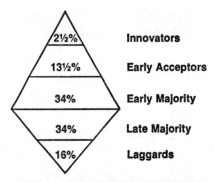

FIGURE 2 THE ADOPTION PROCESS

The diffusion of a product, the process of how a new product is accepted, can be best shown in Figure 2.

It should be noted that the 2½% group of the population who are innovators, people who have a sensitivity and a willingness to accept newness, is not of real importance to the buyer, and too small for significant economic value. The timing of this group's acceptance is often too early to bring immediate commercial value. Additionally, this group is not considered as opinion leaders for the later acceptors who obviously are in greater numbers. The group that sets the path for broader fashion acceptance is the early acceptors, the people most admired and respected.

The dynamics of fashion is shown in Figure 3 which shows the relationship of:

1. The movement of fashion
2. The acceptance by groups
3. The price levels

Figure 3 points out average conditions and attitudes of consumers, stores, price, and movement. It must be noted, for example, that there are chain stores that stock high priced merchandise and some fashions rise from the lowest prices. Blue jeans and nylon sweaters are two classifications of merchandise that received early acceptance at modest prices and eventually rose to broader acceptance at higher price levels. As a merchandising principle therefore, fashion is not a price. However, new fashions often start at higher prices and then trickle down to acceptance by wider segments of the population at lesser prices. As a merchandising axiom, the penalty for being late is the necessity for being lower priced. When one says, "me too," it does not have promotional "steam" as a motivating force. Many department store buyers are given the following credo:

- Our store does not want to be a fast first.
- We do want to be a fast second.
- You will be fired for being a slow third.

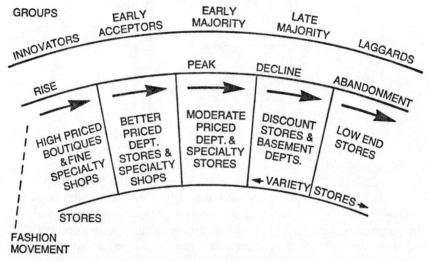

FIGURE 3 THE DYNAMICS OF FASHION

One additional thought before the discussion of other characteristics of fashion. In a world of instantaneous communication and technological speed, fashion "knock offs" are often available at the same time as originals. So, despite theories and practices, a buyer must be alert to possible fashion availability at every price level and acceptance by almost all income level groups at the same time.

THE CONSUMER OBSOLESCENCE FACTOR IN FASHION

The term *consumer obsolescence* is usually defined as the rejection of present ownership in favor of something newer even though the old can still be utilized. In an affluent society people are able to practice this luxury which makes for a condition of mass acceptance of mass production.

Manufacturers and fashion merchandisers are continually offering new styles to consumers for the purpose of "aging" their wardrobes. Obsolescence is therefore largely psychological, in the mind of the customer, who buys the new and discards the old. If this factor were not practiced, the fashion industry would not have been able to sell over $70 billion at retail in 1976.

One of the principles of fashion is that it is synonomous with *change.* When there is little change, there is less business; when changes are significant and well accepted by customers, business booms.

INFLUENCES OF CONSUMER ACCEPTANCE OF FASHION

The reasons for buying clothing are manifold and a complete study in itself. The most obvious reason is the protection from the elements. But, in addition to that basic reason one must make the generalization that the purchase is directed towards the search for a state of betterment. Betterment can involve, among other reasons, the desire to express:

1. Social position
2. Authority
3. Wealth
4. Dignity
5. Formality
6. A second "skin" as an improvement on nature
7. Conformity to peer groups and social acceptance
8. Attitudes of conformity—rebellion, etc.
9. Sexual desirability
10. Religious attitudes
11. Esthetic value

The broadest attitudes that affect people are:

1. Economics
2. Social values
3. Cultural values
4. Technology
5. Political activities

We previously defined fashion as a luxury when the obsolescence factor is practiced, and that is the truth. The need is largely created and is psychologically based.

Social activities and values determine what is to be worn for different occasions. Multiplicity of social occasions require different, appropriate costumes that are accepted by peer groups.

Cultural values are long-term artifacts and ideas handed down from generation to generation and reflect what is acceptable on a national as well as sub-cultural basis. Ethnic groups often wear apparel particularly styled for them.

Technological advances have affected the materials of fashion, how it is made, how fast it can be delivered, how it is sold, and most important what is accepted. Television and the jet plane has widened our horizons by bringing instantaneous communication of ideas that once took years to trickle down to the broad base of the population. It is a far cry from the day when information was relayed by newspapers and magazines, and later when motion pictures were added as another dimension to communication.

Political actions can cause cost variations through taxes, exclusion or acceptance of foreign goods, eliminate or control availability during wars, and make marketers conform to certain methods of distribution, all of which has some impact on what we wear.

Within these broad influences are many specific events that motivate the consumer to accept certain styles for fashion.

1. Prominent personalities who are emulated such as entertainers, political figures (social-anticipatory reference group).
2. Major current events
   A. War (political)
   B. Scientific discovery (technological)
   C. Art events (cultural)
   D. Foreign countries in the news (political, cultural and social values)
   E. Current trends of life styles (social)
      (1) Tennis
      (2) Golf
      (3) Travel
      (4) Use of cars
   F. Job security (economic)

Since every country has varying degrees of strengths and weaknesses, and attitudes in the broad areas of the examples cited, the nature and practice will similarly vary. Hence, what is fashion differs with the place, the degree of change, and the range of people who can accept the fashion.

THE ACTIVITIES OF MERCHANDISING

Since profit is the name of the game, the goal of merchandising is apparent. In order to realize a profit, it necessitates three functions:

1. Planning or estimating
2. Buying or procuring
3. Selling or promoting

The main purpose of planning is to strike a proper balance between sales and stock within the guidelines established by management. Effective buying should achieve a stock position that is adequate to customer demand; therefore in sufficient assortment and depth that customers expect in the store when they are ready to purchase. Selling, or promotion, is the activity that helps the movement of goods from the store into the hands of the ultimate consumer.

What is bought, *how* it is bought, *when* it is bought, and *how* it is to be sold, are related to the philosophy of the store. *Who* it is serving and what *retail mix* it uses are the strategies to appeal to that selected group. In all instances, regardless of store type, the merchandising goals are: the right merchandise, in proper quantities, and at the right time.

To put it another way, consumer orientation is knowing what customers want, at what prices, at what time, and in such quantities that they can absorb.

As a corollary to merchandising, the term retailing should be noted because they are often used interchangeably. Merchandising is part of the larger picture of retailing. Retailing concerns itself with all the activities of buying goods at wholesale, selling the goods at retail prices, and performing all the functions to place it in the hands of the ultimate consumer. Some of the activities that are part of retailing are:

- Merchandising
- Selection of location
- Setting up interior design and fixtures
- Credit extension
- Receiving of goods
- Delivery of goods
- Public relations
- Personnel relations

THE UNIQUENESS OF FASHION MERCHANDISING

If we have agreed that the nature of fashion is change involving obsolescence, which is psychological, then we must realize that there are reasons why fashion merchandise has unique "problems":

1. Obsolescence factor
2. Higher markdowns

3. Faster turnover
4. Seasonal factors
5. Sales promotion

The obsolescence practiced by consumers is also part of the merchandiser's life because merchandise that is on the racks too long, or not readily accepted, can lose value rapidly. Intrinsic value may have little relevancy to the price at which it will sell. This leads to high markdowns, which in turn demands a selling rate at a speed that will maintain a healthy stock position—merchandise that is currently wanted. One of the causes of aging is the seasonal consideration. At the beginning of the season merchandise for that period is young, it later becomes middle-aged, and at the end of the season, old-aged. Hence, with five fashion seasons a year, fashion merchandise is in the constant process of aging, to a greater degree than all other kinds of merchandise (without consideration for certain food products). The psychological factor that is an integral part of acceptance, the selling of fashion apparel, must have emotional values beyond that needed for most consumer products. Fashion merchandising is substantively different—always exciting, always changing.

THE MEASURABILITY OF A BUYER OF FASHION APPAREL

Every buyer is charged with meeting store standards. In the case of fashion merchandisers, the standards are often difficult to achieve or maintain because of the intense competition and the capriciousness of consumers whose preferences are hard to fathom before stock investments are made.

Fashion buyers' results are compared to competitive buyers in the trading area, intraorganizationally (member stores of the same corporate entity), on a regional basis (Federal Reserve Bank figures), and sometimes on a national basis.

Specifically, these are the measurement values usually used:

1. Sales (usually expressed as a percentage of gain or loss to the period of comparison)
   A. By units
   B. By dollars
2. Inventory
   A. Stock turnover
   B. Percent shortage to net sales
   C. Old goods vs. new goods

3. Margin Results
   A. Initial markup (difference between cost and original retail)
   B. Gross margin (net sales less cost of goods sold)
   C. Controllable margin (gross margin less direct department expenses)
   D. Operating profit (gross margin less cost of sales and operating expenses

CONCLUSION

The meaning of fashion within the context of our subject is synonomous with acceptance and includes the additional elements of time, place and change. These conditions will be later related to the activities of a buyer—how a budget is planned, how fashion is predicted, and the techniques of purchasing fashion goods.

Case 1
The Men's Wear
Buyer's Frustration

Jim Safford is the buyer of men's suits for the Langley Department Store, Milwaukee, Wisconsin. He has been in this position for five years. He was employed directly after graduation from the University of Michigan, where he earned an M.B.A. After completion of the Langley Training Program, he was an assistant buyer, then an associate, and finally a buyer, all within two years. His first buying assignment was in the Men's Furnishings Department where he performed admirably for four years. His record was so good that management decided to give him the new assignment of buying men's suits, a department that was on the downgrade. Safford felt that this was a step towards a position on the management team. An achievement that would take another year or two. In fact, it was common knowledge among personnel that he was a young man slated for management, so his thoughts were not reveries.

Safford tackled his job with enthusiasm, care and understanding. He gave the opportunity all it was worth—a lifetime career that was going to lead to big things.

Unfortunately, Safford was the victim of circumstance and some of the glitter began to peel. Despite all his efforts that included advice from the resident buying office, peers in the field and friendly manufacturers, business began to sag. The trend towards sportswear hurt his business; losses of volume were suffered up to 10% per year and after five years, the department's projected volume for the next year was 60% of what it was when Safford took over.

Management was not deeply disturbed because they were aware of the fashion trend and had industry records which reflected similar regional and national results.

Despite management's support, Safford was grim and never ceased to search for the key to build the department and again assume the position of a man on the rise.

Finally, during January of this year, the message came across loud and clear. The market, optimistic for the first time in years, reported a trend towards men's suits and a new silhouette, the revival of the double-breasted, English lounge suit. Just what the doctor ordered as medicine to accelerate business.

Safford visited the market and shopped it thoroughly. He spoke to all sources of information—and learned of heavy manufac-

26

turer production concentrating on the new style, stores' plans for strong promotions and fashion magazine support.

He was convinced—this was it. And he made up his mind that 80% of his suit budget should be put behind the trend.

Fortunately, his divisional merchandise manager, Dan Powers, was in the market and was able to meet him for dinner.

An enthusiastic Safford outlined his plan and noted the following:

- Men's suit orders must be given four to six months in advance of delivery.
- The lead time requires an early decision; it is not possible to get "right" once the season starts. Failure to take an early stand means a serious loss during the best selling period of the year.
- The new styling is not revolutionary; it is highly wearable.
- Competition is going all-out for the first good news in years.
- Co-op ad money is available and strong promotional efforts will not exceed last year's budget substantially.
- Customers are looking for styling that is wearable and smart. Moreover, the styling fits right into the Langley customers' taste.

Powers listened carefully and then replied, "It all sounds great; but fashion is acceptance, anything less is an opinion. I suggest that we plan one early strong promotion, about 20% of your open-to-buy, which is an important investment."

Safford was annoyed, "You were a fashion merchandiser of female apparel; you just don't understand the men's business."

One word led to another and an impasse developed.

Both men were angry and finally Powers said, "I've made my decision and I will not countersign any order beyond 20% of the OTB. That is final."

And with those words, he got up from his seat and said, "Good night."

Safford was in a stew. He understood the meaning of fashion and knew the difference between opinion and acceptance. But he also felt that even modest success would bolster the department's sagging volume. In fact, he worked out a chart proving that a markdown of 15% of net sales would still allow for a profitable season. He knew that the department needed stimulation, the store needed newness, and the sales personnel needed the lift of a new fashion development.

He considered going over Powers' head to the general merchandise manager, who was regarded as a logical thinker. His main arguments would be:

- He is a seasoned buyer who should be the selector of merchandise. After all, he is being paid to evaluate the market, study customers and stock merchandise.
- Retailing demands that merchandisers take some risk. Staying with the tried and true does not reflect fashion leadership.
- The element of risk in this case is minute.

Before taking his next step, Safford thought he would discuss the issues with friendly peers. He called you, a buyer of ladies' coats at Langley's, and asked your advice.

"If you were Dan Powers, how would you respond to my plan. I know you're a fashion person and can help me to understand. I really have lost my objectivity."

How would you advise Jim Safford understanding that he is a logical person who requires an incisive analysis of the situation.

Case 2
Customer Segmentation Importance

The United Stores Syndicate is a well-known independent resident buying office with a clientele of two hundred member stores whose yearly sales range from $1 to $5 million. They pride themselves in offering individualized service to their members.

Gorham and Silver, Inc., a member store, is a $5 million operation in Hammond, Indiana. Established seventy-five years ago, it is considered the leading specialty shop of the city, enjoying a reputation for quality men's, ladies' and children's fashions. The charge account list is approximately five thousand and includes fashion leaders and highest income people of the city and suburban areas.

A week ago, Bill Gorham and Arnie Silver made a special trip to New York to meet with James Colton, the president of United Stores Syndicate, to have him settle a dispute.

From their conversation, it was apparent that Bill Gorham, the administrator, is pleased with the operation which yields a 10% profit before taxes, which is better than most stores in the country. He is additionally pleased with the large active group of people who have patronized the store for many years.

Arnie Silver, the general merchandise manager, although satisfied with the profit performance, has a different point of view. He claims that even though the store has successfully met all competition over the years, attrition could set in, because the most important customers range in age from thirty-five to fifty.

Gorham showed statistics proving that the people with the highest incomes are in the thirty-five to fifty group.

"Why fight a strength," he said.

Silver, on the other hand, said, "Look at this picture. Our junior sales are 15% of our total female retail business; our Misses Department yields 60%; and half size business is 25%. This is an unhealthy state; we are catering to the older group that will eventually fade away. The younger people are being weaned to shop at other stores and they will continue to in the years ahead. We have to get on the ball and change our merchandising concept. Our merchandise must look younger, our advertising format should be changed and we should design a series of events to attract the young."

"Hell," said Gorham, "and drive away loyal customers who'll feel left out and uncomfortable in a store taken over by kids who want lights, music, and excitement. We have an investment in time, money, location, and goodwill, all of which nets a handsome return. Gambling is for Las Vegas, not business. The youngsters of today will shop at our store in due time. They know the quality level of what we offer, the services that are tops and the reputation of the store. I'm not worried about tomorrow."

A great deal more was discussed but the foregoing is a gist of the conversation.

You are a member of the buying staff of United Stores Syndicate and were present during the meeting. James Colton has asked you to analyze the situation and detail a report in which you will select a desired route for Gorham and Silver, Inc. to follow.

Case 3
The Impossible Goals

The Norris Department Store of Pittsburgh, Pennsylvania, has an illustrious background. Established eighty years ago, it grew with the city and enjoys a fine reputation as one of the leading stores of the state, doing over $50 million a year on popular- to medium-priced merchandise. Its advertising slogan—*A Complete Store for the Complete Family*—is more than a slogan. The assortment and depth of merchandise and range of prices are more than ample proof of the truth of the slogan.

However, in the ready-to-wear section, the popular-priced dress department—the Miss Gotham Department—did not yield a satisfactory profit.

After promoting several associate buyers to the Miss Gotham Department, with no signal success, management hired a buyer from New York, Joe Turner, thirty-five years old, with a strong background in chain store popular-priced buying. He was given a handsome salary and a bonus arrangement based on volume.

From the beginning, it was apparent that Turner knew the market. He was able to add new resources and "hot" selling styles, build price ranges and increase promotion. In the course of a year and a half, he tacked on a 25% increase in business.

Management, at first, was exceedingly happy. The department was a beehive of activity on most days of the week and on Saturdays, the store looked like a New York subway jam.

After reviewing the records, the general merchandise manager called Phil Forrester, the divisional merchandise manager, up to his office and said, "Phil, Department 345, the Miss Gotham Department, is showing a healthy growth, but I'm concerned. Your buyer certainly has achieved the volume we've been looking for, but at what price. The advertising cost has doubled, the markdowns have gone from 12% to 17%, the cumulative markup from 43% to 40.4% and the turnover rate from 5 to 8½ times a year. It's true that the margin has also increased which is good. I think we better put a brake on Joe Turner before he goes haywire and we end up looking like a chain or discount store."

Accordingly, Phil Forrester called Turner in for a meeting.

He began by saying, "Joe, you've been here almost two years, and you've done a great job. I'm not going to give you statistics, you're a merchant and can read them as well as I can. The time has come to pause and see where we're going. Let's start by reviewing the store, its customers, and the merchandising tactics that are good for a long run."

Turner's immediate reaction was that he was being put on the defensive and replied, "I'm confused. First you want volume and now that you have it, you're unhappy. This hurts. You know that I'm trying to make a career in this store and I want a promotion to divisional merchandise manager. I came in for praise and I hear myself being damned."

"Hold on," said Forrester. "I haven't uttered a word of criticism. All I've said is that we should review where we've been and where we're going."

"I'm listening," Turner responded.

"Here's what we want," the divisional merchandise manager stated. "A slower turnover, about 6½ times; higher initial markup; higher cumulative and maintained markup; and lower markdown rate."

"And less volume," Turner replied.

"If necessary," said Forrester.

The meeting continued during which Forrester assured Turner that he had a place in the store, that management was happy with him and that the meeting was designed to ensure future success.

When Turner went home that night he was disturbed. He could not get it out of his mind that someone was trying to do him harm and that in the long run, he had satisfied no one in higher management. One of his thoughts was that he had earned too much money for the store's comfort and now that a cure for the department had been developed he was being eased out. He had seen this happen. His greatest unhappiness was that he was under the impression that he was doing an excellent job and getting ready to request a promotion; now he was under pressure to hold his job.

He felt he had two alternatives. One, to look for another job, or two, stay at Norris' and if possible, try to do the job management requested.

If you were Joe Turner and selected the latter alternative, what could you do to try to obtain the goals of the general merchandise manager?

III

FASHION BUYING AS A CAREER

Many young people want to become *fashion buyers*. They are part of a large group who believe that a buyer's job is glamorous, that it provides excitement, rapid advancement, and good remuneration. Not all of these people know or realize that the fashion buyer's job also demands long hours and very hard work. They are also unaware that management looks for certain desirable traits, characteristics, and attributes which are believed to help assure success on the job. For example, buyers must be able to:

1. Express themselves easily and fluently both orally and in writing.
2. Think in numbers or in an analytical manner.
3. Get along with their subordinates, their superiors, their peers, their vendors, and their customers.
4. Be enthusiastic, particularly about their merchandise.
5. Develop a sense of curiosity.
6. Be creative.
7. Develop good physical stamina and good emotional stability.
8. Be alert.
9. Have a good memory.
10. Develop a number of managerial skills such as the ability to delegate authority and responsibility; to use time adequately; to be flexible; to be fair, impartial and tactful.

There are several other factors considered important or desirable that management looks for in the selection of fashion buyers: *educational background* and *work experience*.

It is safe to assume that education tailored towards a career in fashion buying and merchandising is becoming the rule rather than the exception. A college education is currently considered to be practically mandatory as an entrance requirement to the field. The amount of college education varies from time to time and from place to place depending upon a variety of factors including the state of the nation's economy.

Previous work experience, such as part-time and summer vacation jobs during high school and college years, is an important factor in selecting candidates for training as potential buyers. The greatest value of such work experience is in selling positions because future buyers can get an early start, while selling, in interpreting customers' wants and needs.

ADVANTAGES AND DISADVANTAGES OF A CAREER IN FASHION BUYING

Buying as a career may also be studied by analyzing both the "pros and cons."

ADVANTAGES

1. Prestige
2. Good pay
3. Relatively rapid advancement
4. Opportunity for economic growth
5. Opportunity for personal growth
6. Opportunity to work almost anywhere—transferability
7. Travel
8. Self-expression
9. A lead to other career opportunities.

DISADVANTAGES

1. Hard work
2. Long hours
3. Pressure
4. Competition
5. Accountability
6. Limitations in advancement
7. Excessive travel
8. Uniformity of the training program

9. Rigidity in the training program as well as in the organization

10. Anti-social forces

Fashion buying and merchandising offers the dedicated individual an opportunity to enjoy a good life in a good career. The rewards are numerous and self-satisfying, but like any other profession or business activity, one must be willing to endure the disadvantages.

Case 4
Terri's Tearful Tale

Terri Hall, as long as she could remember, always wanted to be a fashion buyer. In high school, she not only pursued a career in distributive education but she was also an active member of D.E.C.A., both on a state and national level. Upon graduating from high school, she enrolled in one of the country's best known junior colleges which had the largest fashion merchandising program in the country. While in college, she made excellent grades as well as being elected president of the Merchandising Society. And upon graduation, she was awarded the coveted Benjamin-Grossman prize, which provided the winner with a trip to Europe to attend the Paris fall fashion openings.

Terri's career continued with unusual progress. After her return from Europe, she assumed a position as an executive trainee at Rogers Department Store, one of New York City's best run and most successful stores. She was promoted to the position of assistant buyer of basement children's wear before the year was up and then was advanced again to the position of department manager at the new Huntington store. Terri Hall returned to the main store as buyer of basement children's wear when her former boss, Ethel Conrad, retired. Conrad recommended Terri for that position. Thus, at the age of twenty-three, Terri had not only reached her life's goal, but she was also the youngest buyer in Rogers' recent history.

It was true that the Basement Children's Wear Department was not a large one but it was a step in the right direction. Terri Hall was a buyer in an outstanding store with the opportunity to advance to the position of divisional merchandise manager in the basement, or perhaps to become a buyer in the upstairs store.

Like many of her contemporaries, Terri Hall had a fond place in her heart for the college that she felt had provided her with the principal means of achieving her goal. Accordingly, she kept in touch with the chairperson and various members of the Fashion Merchandising Department; served on industry panels as a guest speaker; and took as active a role in alumni affairs as her job permitted.

One day, one of her former instructors with whom Hall had maintained close contact, Professor Pierce Arrow, received a phone call from her requesting an appointment. At the duly appointed time, Terri appeared at Professor Arrow's office. They exchanged greetings and pleasantries, and suddenly she burst into tears.

When he finally calmed her down, Professor Arrow inquired, "My goodness, Terri, why the tears? You're an attractive, well groomed, poised woman. You're one of our most successful, recent graduates. You're a full-fledged buyer with one of the country's largest and outstanding merchandising firms, and you're not even twenty-four years old. Do I have to gild the lily any more? What brought that flood on?"

"Professor Arrow, you're the only one I can talk to," Terri replied. "You've met my folks . . . they're from the old country and don't know the modern business world. . . ."

"Continue," said Professor Arrow.

"I should be the happiest person in the world. All my life I wanted to be a buyer and now that I am one, I can't cope . . . I'm so miserable (more tears) . . . I want to throw the whole thing away, and I'm ashamed to tell anyone else about it," she said.

"This just doesn't make sense. It can't be that bad," Professor Arrow said. "Give me the whole story from the beginning."

"Well," began Terri slowly, "I'm completely exhausted physically and emotionally. I have no assistant because my department is too small. I have to be all over the floor; in the receiving room. Management is paying my fees towards a Bachelor's Degree so I'm going to school at least two nights week, but I love school. I work late every Thursday night and sometimes take paper work home over the weekends. And you know what it's like to prepare for big promotions such as Back-to-School or Get-Ready-for-Camp. And those five to six weeks before Christmas . . . forget it. When I get home at night, I'm so exhausted that I frequently fall asleep with my clothes on. I don't even find time to eat right and I live mostly on fast foods, junk food and coke which I gobble up between rushing around. I have no time for a social life, in fact, I haven't had a date for six months (tears) and for a young girl like me that's awful (more tears). I even turn down dinners and theatre tickets from my manufacturers. It's just too much for me."

This conversation went on for the better part of an hour. When Terri left Professor Arrow's office, she was dry-eyed and smiling. She now felt that all was not lost.

If you were Professor Pierce Arrow, what advice would you give Terri Hall to help save her career in fashion buying.

Case 5
The Executive Trainee

Baird's Department Store is generally regarded in the trade as one of the best managed stores in the West Coast metropolitan area in which it is located. And Baird's customers sing its praises in regard to both merchandise and service. All in all, a real winner. Well, not entirely. The rotten apple spoiling the barrel was the Boys' Wear Department in the newest Baird branch store located in the suburb of Clinton.

Philip Jensen was this branch store's Boys' Wear Department manager. Phil had been an assistant buyer in men's shoes at the main store following his stint as a member of Baird's famous Executive Training Squad. His promotion to branch store department manager followed the normal Baird hierarchy pattern which ordained that if Philip Jensen did a good job at Clinton, he would, at the proper time, return to the main store as a buyer.

As the first department manager in a new store, it was Jensen's style to be known as a "good boss," loved by his entire staff of sales- and stockpeople. An easygoing person naturally, his staff soon learned to take advantage of him. And as a result, it was not long before the department began to suffer.

To the trained eye, the Boys' Wear Department was a mess. Related merchandise was never in the same area; signs were frequently missing and incorrect; stockrooms were sloppy and disorganized creating delays or missed sales because salespeople could not find merchandise when needed.

Salespeople became too haughty to do stockwork, and the stockpeople were too busy "goofing off." Jensen allowed his staff to take long lunch hours and stretch their breaks. It was also common for them to shop in the store any time they felt so inclined. All of which made floor coverage a generally haphazard thing, at best.

Jensen was not entirely unaware of these matters but by now it was practically too late to do anything about what the department personnel now regarded as their rights, not as privileges. Phil rationalized this general disregard of discipline by telling himself that the salespeople turn in such excellent tallies every day . . . if I tighten up now, their sales will probably drop off and then I'll be in trouble. . . .

However, such conditions never pass unnoticed and both the Clinton store manager, Jack Rose, and Philip Jensen's divisional group manager, Jim Santos, were aware of the personnel situation in the Boys' Wear Department. Jim Santos, feeling a partial sense of guilt for allowing Jensen to fall so deeply into this quagmire, persuaded Jack Rose to join him in recommending that Jensen be transferred instead of eliminating him. Rose, however, insisted on dictating a long memorandum to Philip Jensen detailing his apparent lack of leadership.

Lester Siegler, an assistant buyer of men's furnishings at the main store, was promoted to the Clinton store as the new Boys' Wear Department manager. Because he had made previous arrangements to go on his honeymoon, there was a delay in the time that he was able to take over the department.

During these several weeks, the supervision of the Boys' Wear Department fell nominally to Santos, but actually two of the senior salespeople of the Boys' Wear Department divided the job. This only made matters worse and the department became even more disorganized. As an example of this chaos, the salespeople took as many as three or four breaks a day instead of the one permitted.

When Lester Siegler finally arrived at the Clinton store, he first had to orient himself with the stock and department books and acquaint himself with the staff. He also became aware of the fact that he had to play the role of a manager setting up a department from scratch. As a result, he rarely had time to supervise the floor, the most acute problem of the department.

Suddenly, a veritable miracle occurred. The Executive Development Director of Baird's assigned a member of the Executive Training Squad to Lester Siegler's department at Clinton. Up to this time, executive trainees had been assigned only to departments in the main store. Now, the trainees, during their job rotation period, were assigned to branches as well.

Henry Levy, a graduate of a local community college's merchandising program, and regarded by the Executive Training Squad personnel as an "eager beaver," lived near the Clinton suburb and was happy to draw his first assignment as an assistant to Lester Siegler in the Boys' Wear Department. Hank, as he was soon called, was, of course, anxious to do well on his first supervisory assignment. He was sharp, bright, and it took him no time at all to realize and define the problem existing in the department. While Hank felt that something had to be done to tighten up the discipline in the department, he also realized that he had no real authority as an executive trainee. He therefore made it his business to tactfully inform Siegler how he had analyzed the situation that existed in the department and skillfully led his boss into planning what could be done to improve matters.

What would you do if you were in Lester Siegler's place? Outline what you believe Henry Levy suggested as the means to remedy the situation.

CHAPTER
IV

COMMON KNOWLEDGE FOR FASHION BUYERS

The previous chapter dealt with the requirements and characteristics most needed by a trainee to secure an entry job in fashion buying. This chapter will detail the areas of knowledge required by fashion buyers, in general, which can be secured by both training and on-the-job work experience. These training programs vary in buying organizations but depend primarily on the size of the operation for scope and sophistication.

1. The Formal Program—includes classroom activities and work assignments in various parts of the organization.
2. On-the-Job Training—the trainee is assigned to a beginner's job in a specific department and learns from the department head as well as the other department employees by working directly with them.
3. Job Rotation—the trainee is moved from job to job and department to department in accordance with a predetermined schedule in order to get a wide view of the total operation.

WHAT IS A BUYER GENERALLY EXPECTED TO KNOW?

PRODUCT KNOWLEDGE

Obviously, every buyer must know the product with which he is dealing. In fashion buying, this means the buyer must know four primary elements of fashion merchandise:

1. Silhouette
2. Texture
3. Color
4. Details

It should be noted that product knowledge is a vast subject area because of modern textile technology which has and can produce a tremendous variety of yarns and fabrics. What fabrics cost, how they perform and how they are suited for specific garments are but a few areas of what the buyer needs to know.

FASHION DYNAMICS AND PRINCIPLES

This is an area that requires both knowledge and intuition because fashion movement is an evolutionary process. If the store is a fashion leader, the merchandise is needed at the first step—the rise. Other stores can enter the evolutionary cycle at the second step— the peak. The timing depends on the store's fashion goals and its relationship to its customers.

The following are some general fashion principles that expert fashion buyers know and understand:

1. Fashion is evolution.
2. Fashion is cyclical.
3. Customers make fashion.
4. Acceptance levels of fashion vary (fad, fashion, classic).
5. Different fashion for different customers (young vs. mature styles).
6. Price is *not* fashion.
7. Nature of fashion is *change.*
8. Fashion reflects life styles.
9. The greatest error of fashion merchandising is to be out of trend.
10. Fashion does not improve with age.

In other words, fashion is for people and their acceptance of it is really what it is all about.

KNOWLEDGE OF THE CUSTOMER

The buyer is not only a people watcher but his knowledge of his customers must be constantly renewed and re-evaluated. It is relatively easy for the professional buyer to keep up-to-date by using *demographical* information—statistics about people or groups involving age, income, education, ethnic backgrounds, etc. But in this day and age, the buyer must also understand *psychographics*—opinions, attitudes, beliefs, etc. held by the customers. Everyone in today's life style seems to be playing a variety of roles and it is the fashion buyer's job to interpret these psychographical expressions and accommodate the actors—the customers—by offering suitable *costumes.*

The buyer must understand that the crux of fashion is change, because people change, and that to discern this change he must constantly study the customer to understand what people do and what they will wear to do it. Thus, a buyer must be involved in life; read newspapers and periodicals; watch television; attend the movies and events whose audience include his customers or potential customers.

SOURCES OF SUPPLY

Fashion markets are located in many cities of the United States, but New York City is undoubtedly the biggest and most important. There are publications and guides published which list manufacturers for every classification of fashion merchandise. There are even booklets which list the occupants of specific buildings in New York City.

However, knowing what manufacturers make what garments and at what price is not enough. Each store (and thus every buyer) must build its own list of merchandise resources that best serves its purposes.

The resident buying office is another valuable resource for merchandise/vendor information (see Chapter VIII).

Obviously, it is relatively simple to secure resource information. The professional buyer is one who knows how to best use the ones best suited for his store and his customers. It is the buyer's job to search, evaluate, select, negotiate and review resources to establish profitable relationships.

MANAGEMENT GOALS AND POLICIES

Of course, when the buyer (or trainee) begins his employment, the goals and policies of the organization are made clear to him. Stores that use mass merchandising techniques such as price appeals or higher-priced stores using designer names, etc. are examples of a *marketing mix* which tries to appeal to and attract a desired segment of customers to that store.

This marketing mix usually includes elements such as the store's location, layout and other physical aspects; the store's merchandising policies on assortments, depth of stock, prices and timing, services; the store's communications to its customers.

It is quite simple to establish the differences in marketing techniques by visiting and observing such differences in fine specialty stores, discount stores, department stores, apparel chain stores, etc. The policies that distinguish one from the other would affect such merchandise aspects as:

1. Price levels (or price points)
2. Price zones (price levels or ranges of greatest importance)
3. Assortment and depth of stock
4. Markup and markdown
5. When, how, what and why (to) promote merchandise

Once top management has decided on which segment of the customer market it wishes to capture, its policies, strategies, and tactics will endeavor to obtain maximum results. The fashion buyer, once made aware of these policies and goals, must stay within the parameters set by management.

BUSINESS MERCHANDISE MATHEMATICS

As previously indicated in Chapter III, a buyer must have a facility in the use of number in order to understand those relationships that are based on mathematics. Since all successful business is based on making a profit, the ability to "think in numbers" is essential. Merchandising mathematics revolves around the use of percentages in order to be able to establish norms that are easy to figure and to evaluate in ratio. Among the important areas in merchandising that require a knowledge of mathematical relationships are:

1. Markup and maintained markup
2. Markdown
3. Gross margin
4. Stock turnover
5. Stock/sales ratio
6. Stock plans
7. Sales plans
8. Dollar and unit control

It is important that the trainee must become aware of the knowledge that begins on the first day of employment. Professional knowledge is gained on-the-job. How long it takes to absorb depends on the level of achievement and the opportunities afforded in a career in fashion buying.

Case 6
Tying One On

Kendall's Department Store is located in a Midwest metropolis and caters to an upper-middle income clientele. In all the departments, and particularly in the ones dealing with fashion merchandise, the buyers are under constant orders from the general merchandise manager, and especially from their divisional merchandise managers, to be on the lookout for highly original, exclusive merchandise. Dusenberry McGrath, the general merchandise manager, has made it a practice to have all such merchandise labeled either *Made Exclusively for Kendall's* or *Designed Exclusively for Kendall's*.

One of McGrath's favorite departments (where he is a big customer at 40% off) is the Men's Furnishings Department. While Kenneth Mackey is the divisional merchandise manager for men's and boys' wear, McGrath himself keeps a close eye on many of the merchandise segments in the Men's Furnishings Department because of his own personal shopping preferences. McGrath is forever sending Frank Dalewood, the men's furnishings buyer, memos, clippings, ads, etc., all intended to prod Dalewood into investigating and buying new lines or styles. It is a ticklish situation for both Mackey and Dalewood.

One of McGrath's chief contributions to the Men's Furnishings Department is his encouragement of buying from relatively unknown designers, especially in the area of men's ties. These designers were usually young and ambitious who generally did well with Kendall's. Probably selling the best in this designed-exclusively-for-Kendall's merchandise is Ricky Rustan. McGrath is one of the most avid collectors of Rustan's originally designed ties.

When Rustan began to sell exclusively to Kendall's, he charged the store $7.50 each for his ties, an item which Dalewood retailed for $15.00. As Rustan's ties increased in popularity, he raised his prices by $1 each and the store passed on this increase to their customers who did not seem to mind paying higher prices for these one-of-a-kind creations. By the end of Rustan's second year with Kendall's, customers were paying $20 per tie.

Now, halfway into his third year as an exclusive Kendall's designer-resource, Rustan is getting restive, even if he is demanding, and getting $11 for the ties which were now still selling quite well at $22 each. He has had many offers to sell his ties to Kendall's competitors under his own name and obtain a wider, healthier distribution for increased volume.

Accordingly, Rustan laid the cards on the table to Dalewood and said that the alternative is a substantial increase in the cost to make up for the lost potential volume.

Dalewood considers the Rustan merchandise valuable both to the store and to his department, but he wonders if his customers finding another price increase, and a substantial one at that, will still continue to buy Rustan's ties. Losing, or sharing a successful manufacturer, the other track, is not an appealing one.

If you were Frank Dalewood, in view of the above, what would you do?

Case 7
The Cashmere Sweater

Sue Robertson is the sweater buyer for Lamont's Department Store which is located in the northern part of the Midwest. Lamont's caters to a lower-middle income clientele and does it quite well.

Robertson is a bit perplexed when she recognizes an early trend of the return of the cashmere sweater to popularity. A quick survey of the import market indicated that $60 retail was about the average price available and Robertson knew that Lamont's regular customers would not go for a $60 sweater—it was out of their price range, even for gift giving. However, she decided that on her forthcoming European buying trip, she would try to develop her own line of cashmere sweaters at a price. She felt, if she could do so in view of this very strongly developing trend, she would have a great addition to her department's volume.

In early February, her first stop in Europe was Hawick, Scotland, where she surveyed the Pringle, Lyle, and Scott lines. As she suspected, the Scottish manufacturers could not beat the $60 retail price. Her last stop in Europe was Perugia, Italy, where she had a number of major Italian knit resources with whom she had made many previous deals and promotions. The entire area was one of highly skilled knitters who had excellent machinery and technical knowledge. Robertson had some very good previous experience in developing specification merchandise in this area.

Sue Robertson sought out the Giovanni Opa Company, one of her best resources in Perugia, and told Signor Bernardo Opa, the firm's president, that she wanted a cashmere sweater in twenty-one gauge to be made up mostly in cardigans, in the basic colors, for year-round selling in her cool climate trading area; plus at least two fashion colors for the forthcoming fall season. Bernardo Opa assured her that his plant could make all the cashmere sweaters she wanted and to her specifications.

The gleeful buyer left Opa an order for $200,000 at retail, subject to confirmation on her return to the United States. Most of the sweaters were to be cardigans to retail at $40—a full $20 below the current U.S. market price. She also rounded out the order by including some long sleeve slip-ons to retail for $30 and some short sleeve slip-ons to retail for $20. Even at these prices, she was able to secure a markup of 50% instead of her regular 45%.

Robertson returned to Lamont's in a semi-delirious state of euphoric happiness. This excitement was transmitted to her divisional merchandise manager, George Goodfellow, and other members of top management at Lamont's, when she described the coup she had scored. Goodfellow not only countersigned the order, but he also had a series of advertisements prepared of twelve-hundred lines each and made a mental note for a four-color, full-page ad for the holiday selling season.

Since Lamont's is located in a cool climate area, Robertson had arranged for the merchandise to be shipped in April—May rather than the normal June—July period.

The first advertisement broke in time for the Mother's Day promotion and it was a smash hit—the biggest single day in the Sportswear Department's history. The cashmere sweaters at-a-price took the city by storm. Lamont's competitors had their sweaters at the $60 retail and they were stuck with present inventory. In addition, they had not yet received their new stock and Lamont's had actually caught them flat-footed by the early delivery arranged by Sue Robertson.

Robert Stevens, sportswear buyer for Kahn's Department Store, Lamont's principal competitor, could not believe what he was witnessing. He therefore sent one of his salespeople over to Lamont's to purchase one of the $40 cardigans to see for himself. He weighed the sweater, and it checked out as a five and a half pound garment just like his $60 ones. The workmanship was fine—it was made on full-fashion machines. But with his own divisional merchandise manager riding his back, Stevens had to "smell a rat" to stay alive. So, at the first opportunity he took the sweater to New York with him on a buying trip and went to see one of his good friends in the sweater business.

This man was primarily a yarn expert and when he had the sweater in his hands, he said simply, "Of course this is a $40 sweater. It's 15% nylon and not 100% cashmere as labeled!"

Stevens went home humming a happy tune. First, he "leaked" the story to the fashion editor of the city's leading newspaper. Then he had one of his friends file a complaint with the Better Business Bureau. Finally, he ran an ad on his own cashmere sweaters which trumpeted the following message:

OUR SWEATERS ARE 100% PURE CASHMERE
THERE IS NO NYLON IN OUR CASHMERE SWEATERS

The combination of the Better Business Bureau's investigation, the feature story on the fashion page of *The Sentinel-Times Gazette*, and the implications of the Kahn Department Store's ad, sent waves of horror throughout Lamont's.

Dewayne Lamont, great-grandson of the founder and currently president of the store, called George Goodfellow to his office and gave him "Hail, Columbia, Happy Land!" He pointed out that not only was the entire store's reputation going down the drain but also a great deal of the goodwill that was built up in the community would vanish into thin air.

"The public," Lamont screamed, "will never believe us any more . . . we are suspects from now on."

Of course, Sue Robertson is in big trouble in many ways. She has a huge investment in the Opa sweaters. All future ads, and the merchandise itself, will have to indicate the nylon content. This will depress the value of the sweater considerably. Many customers who have already bought the sweaters will probably return them for credit or refund.

In view of the Lamont's president's anger, and the divisional merchandise manager's disgust, what should Sue Robertson say and do?

Case 8
The New
Lingerie Buyer

Siegel's was one of the original, and is still, a leading, underselling fashion merchandise store in metropolitan New York City. During the period of amalgamation, acquisition, and merger that the country has recently emerged from, Siegel's was acquired by one of the world's largest oil companies as a hedge against a potential loss of revenue in the event of another disastrous Middle East oil boycott. While the new parent company announced to the press, to the public and, of course, to Siegel's personnel that there would be no changes in Siegel's policies, procedures, and personnel, the old management soon began to feel both subtle and overt pressures from Houston, Texas, the oil company's headquarters.

In fact, Jack Siegel, the president of Siegel's, received a communique from national headquarters informing him that the board of directors had reviewed the Siegel operation at their last meeting. They had come to the conclusion that a gradual, department-by-department, upward revision of its fashion image was needed. The oil company executives wanted Siegel's to eventually discard the cheap, bargain basement atmosphere of the store and emerge as a quality store.

Siegel's has been in business in New York City for over seventy-five years. Its founder, Mendel Siegel, had given up his pushcart on Hester Street and had taken a small store "uptown" on 14th Street, at the end of World War I. He bought cheap and sold cheap and over the years, this penny business had become a multi-million dollar enterprise that had finally caught the eye of the Wall Street brokers who were looking for promising diversifications for oil cartels, food processing giants, Arab sheiks, Greek shipping tycoons, et al. The idea of upgrading Siegel's to a Fifth Avenue fashion store seemed somewhat ludicrous to Jack Siegel, but he was now a salaried employee with a fantastically secure, ten year financial deal and all he did was shrug his shoulders and go back to work.

One way to change your image department-by-department is to bring in new buyers with Fifth Avenue or similar store experience. The first opportunity to do so occurred when Alicia McElvaney, the lingerie buyer, retired under the new liberal pension plan instituted by the new owners. To replace McElvaney, Siegel's hired Myra

Block, luring her away from her famous Fifth Avenue store by means of a huge salary and bonus arrangement on a long-term contract. In her former position, Block bought merchandise that sold, for example, in nightgowns from $25 to $100; at Siegel's, the price range for nightgowns in the Lingerie Department was from $5 to $15. While Block was given the long-range goal of raising Siegel's lingerie selections both in price range and quality, she still had to contend with present conditions. She was well aware of the fact that you just can't come in, get rid of all the old, cheap merchandise and bring in new, higher-priced, better quality goods. It would be a gradual merchandising process, that would involve redecorating and refixturing the department (and probably the floor), and re-training and replacing the department personnel.

Myra Block's immediate concern was today's business. She knew she first had to deal with the Lingerie Department's current resources, who were all new to her because they were in a much lower-priced market than she was accustomed to buying in. Her first goal was to get these manufacturers, or similar ones, to improve the quality, appearance and delivery of their merchandise. To add to her difficulties, one of the department's chief resources, Omega Lingerie, had just been sold to a conglomerate whose principal products included motorcycles and speedboats—never apparel, let alone lingerie manufacturing. Omega was finding it very difficult under their new management to give good delivery; and their workmanship, which had never been good, had now become quite inferior.

As a new buyer, Block was reluctant to bring any new resources into the store at this stage of the game; and she was especially unfamiliar with the lower-priced lingerie market. In her dilemma, she was uncertain whether any new, unfamiliar resources she could select would do any better.

What would you advise Myra Block to do?

THE ORGANIZATION OF A LARGE RETAIL STORE

There can be little contradiction to the statement that the common goal of all business is to make a profit. It follows therefore that all business in order to insure this profit must be structured so that the jobs involved are performed well.

Before the advent of the large store, the proprietor of the small store was responsible for running the entire store (Chapter IX). But when the organization is large, it is necessary to assign *authority* and to delegate the *responsibility* of running the business to professionals who can be held *accountable* for a profitable operation.

The above theory of organization evidently was not heeded by the "growing-like-Topsy" retail firms in the United States during the first quarter of the twentieth century. Because of this, the National Retail Dry Goods Association (N.R.D.G.A.), now known as the National Retail Merchants Association (N.R.M.A.), the industry's most important trade organization, sponsored an investigation. The purpose of this study was to determine the cause of the widespread poor profit picture in so many large retail organizations as compared to industrial organizations of a similar size and scope. The gist of the report was published as a book in 1927 by banker-economist Paul Mazur under the title *Principles of Organization Applied to Modern Retailing.* This book, which became a classic in its field, revolves around the primary thesis that large retail stores were badly organized or had no real organization at all. A proposed, typical organization structure which became known as "The Mazur Plan" was included in this book and had a tremendous influence on the industry.

"The Mazur Plan" urged large retail stores to organize themselves on a solid foundation which was based upon the then well-known four major functions of the store:

1. Merchandising
2. Sales Promotion
3. Control
4. Operations

While it was soon discovered that "The Mazur Plan" had a number of built-in errors (particularly where it split the authority over the store's salespeople between the Merchandising and the Operations Divisions, giving them two supervisors where one was surely enough), it did pave the way for better organized stores. However, in 1959, the N.R.M.A. realized that as the leading industry spokesman they had an obligation to upgrade "The Mazur Plan" in light of not only its discernible mistakes, but also in view of advances in distribution which had occurred since the original report was issued. After careful research by one of the nation's top professional management consulting firms, a new report was issued which substituted a new *line* and *staff* organization for the old Mazur Plan's *line* structure.

The following is a brief analysis of the four-division line organization structure based on "The Mazur Plan":

1. *Merchandising Division*
   A. Headed by a General Merchandise Manager.
   B. Responsibility delegated to a group of divisional merchandise managers, each of whom is in charge of a group of departments that are generally related.
   C. Each divisional merchandise manager supervises a number of buyers, each of whom heads a merchandise department.
   D. Functions:
      (1) Planning
      (2) Buying
      (3) Pricing
      (4) Promotion
      (5) Selling
2. *Sales Promotion Division*
   A. Headed by a Sales Promotion Manager.
   B. Has three main departments related to the three main functions of the division:

      (1) Advertising
      (2) Display
      (3) Public relations
  3. *Control Division*
    A. Headed by the Controller.
    B. Primary functions include:
      (1) Accounting
      (2) Credit and collections
      (3) Merchandise statistics
  4. *Operations Division*
    A. Headed by the Store Manager.
    B. Many functions—all involving the operations of the store:
      (1) Delivery, wrapping and packing
      (2) Maintenance
      (3) Receiving, marking, warehousing, and traffic
      (4) Protection
      (5) Work rooms and alteration areas
      (6) Supplies
      (7) Customer services

In addition to the four original divisions of "The Mazur Plan," many large stores have added two others:

  1. *Personnel Division*
    A. Headed by a Personnel Director.
    B. Usually consists of three departments:
      (1) Employment
      (2) Training
      (3) Employee services
  2. *Branch Stores Division*
    A. Headed by a Manager or Vice President for Branch Stores.
    B. The individual branch stores usually have three major departments:
      (1) Operations
      (2) Personnel
      (3) Merchandising and sales

"The Mazur Plan," whether it consists of the original four divisions or includes a fifth and a sixth division is organized entirely as a *line* organization. In fact, there are only three actual line divisions—buying, promoting, and managing. These are the divisions that perform functions involved in the actual distribution of goods.

Thus, the Control Division and the Personnel Division are in reality *staff* organizations—they assist the *line* divisions to do a better job by advising, reviewing, recommending, etc.

A BRIEF ANALYSIS OF THE LINE AND STAFF PLAN

The relatively newer N.R.D.G.A. proposal, recommending a review and a revision of "The Mazur Plan," may be broken down into two simple parts:

1. Three *line* organizations
    A. Merchandising Division
    B. Operations Division
    C. Sales Division
        (1) Personal selling
        (2) Sales promotion
            (a) Advertising
            (b) Display
            (c) Public relations
2. Two *staff* organizations
    A. Personnel
    B. Control

BRANCH STORES

The post-World War II population explosion which led to the growth, development, and expansion of large suburban areas of all major United States cities, also created the need for the large retail stores of these cities to move to these new suburbs with their customers.

While there is some credence given to the belief that the branch store movement is still in its formative stages and therefore still subject to change, we can classify them into three major types.

THE BASIC MAIN STORE SYSTEM

The basic main store system is commonly known as the "Brood Hen and Chick" method. Under this system, the main store controls the relatively small branches which are usually close to the mother store (the main store) in all phases of merchandising as well as in operations.

THE MULTI-UNIT SYSTEM

The multi-unit system gives the branches more autonomy, because there is a good possibility that the branches are almost as large as the main store and that they are probably at a considerable distance from it. There is also a good chance that the multi-unit system is being used because there are so many branches that the main store buyer just cannot handle all the work that the basic main store system described above entails.

In any event, under the multi-unit system, some departments in the branch store might even have their own buyers. More commonly, however, while the main store buyer is in charge, he acts more as a merchandise manager, while the branch store department manager has a varied amount of autonomy in merchandise selection, reorder, preparation of sales promotion events, etc.

THE CENTRALIZED ADMINISTRATION SYSTEM

The centralized administration system is used in those stores that have many branches and that are in reality almost a chain. The main store buyer is primarily concerned with buying and merchandising. In fact, there are large stores such as Macy's, New York City, whose buyers operate from central buying offices and are not directly involved with the floor selling or activity, which is the responsibility of a sales promotion department.

SUPPORTIVE STAFF SERVICES

There are a number of staff services that assist the buyer in the large department store in making better buying and merchandising decisions.

THE FASHION OFFICE

The Fashion Office is headed by a Fashion Coordinator or Fashion Director, whose work entails collecting fashion information and summarizing this information for use by merchandising and sales promotion executives and sales force; planning, directing, and producing a variety of fashion shows. The fashion office attempts to produce a coordinated fashion image for the store.

THE UNIT CONTROL OFFICE

The Unit Control Office gathers information from sales tags, sales slips, stock figures, etc. It furnishes the buyer with daily information on inventory, sales results, merchandise receipts, etc. This information is used by the buyer to determine his merchandising and buying transactions.

THE COMPARISON OFFICE

The Comparison Office is an independent staff of shoppers whose primary job is to check the various departments of their own store and compare their merchandise, stock assortments, prices, etc. to competitive stores. The results of these investigations are reported to the general merchandise manager. In addition to this actual comparison work, these shoppers frequently bring in new or different merchandise they may have found in other stores.

THE TESTING AND STANDARDS OFFICE

The Testing and Standards Office is maintained only by the largest stores because of the expense in organizing and maintaining a staff of experts as well as costly equipment; other merchandising organizations use the services of outside commercial or college laboratories for testing merchandise. In either case, this office helps the buyer to set specifications and standards for vendors; helps to develop new products (not including style ideas for apparel buyers) or improve existing ones; helps to keep sales promotion claims in line; and tests merchandise for defects to avoid trouble with the public.

THE RESEARCH OFFICE

The Research Office is maintained only by the largest stores, because it is an expensive, albeit worthwhile undertaking, among whose possible research activities would include: population and income studies for new branch store locations; store layout designs; traffic studies of customers in both store or individual departments; analysis of statistical data from the store's own merchandising and operation activities; formulate or revise systems and procedures, forms.

THE RESIDENT BUYING OFFICE

The Resident Buying Office is dealt with in detail in Chapter VIII. It is included here as a supportive staff service in both the figurative as well as the literal sense because its activities, insofar as assisting the buyer in arriving at better merchandising and buying decisions, are truly helpful even though it is an external source of information.

MANAGEMENT OF MERCHANDISE ACTIVITIES

There are four principal non–merchandising activities involved in the daily handling of fashion goods that are part of many buyers' jobs, particularly in the large store:

1. *Traffic*

    The buyer has a responsibility when he is executing a purchase order for merchandise to specify thereon the means of transportation of the merchandise from the vendor to the store in the fastest, safest, and most inexpensive method possible. This responsibility arises from the fact that the cost of transporting the merchandise is usually borne by the store and must be added to the cost of the goods. Large stores have a Traffic (Management) Department which is part of the Receiving Department.

2. *Receiving*

    Once the merchandise is ordered and the shipping/traffic instructions issued, the buyer must await the arrival of his merchandise at the store. It will be delivered to the Receiving Department to be checked for gross amount; checked against the buyer's order for style, sizes, prices, colors, etc.; inspected for shortages or damages; and then prepared for price marking. (Some larger stores employ a carrier that receives and marks goods, e.g. Posner.)

3. *Marking*

    It is the buyer's responsibility to give the marking room personnel complete information necessary for the price tag. The buyer should check to see that not only are the prices accurate but that the encoded information such as vendor, color, style number are correct for later use by the Unit Control Office.

4. *Distribution*

    The final step in these non-merchandising activities

related to buying is getting the received, checked, and marked merchandise to the selling floor or the department's stock areas. The distribution of this merchandise to branch stores in accordance with previously devised plans is another aspect of this distribution function. The buyer's responsibility is to decide how a constant flow of merchandise is to be handled and to give instructions which will not only prevent congestion in these non-selling areas of the store, but to get the merchandise settled according to plan.

Case 9
Stockwork:
The Buyer's Bane

Bridge's is the largest department store in the northwestern city in which it is located. It is well known in a large trading area for its good merchandise and excellent customer service. One of Bridge's most active and profitable departments is its Misses Dress Department whose buyer, Cynthia Matthews, is regarded by her superiors as someone definitely on her way up.

Matthews is a bright, young career woman, just turned twenty-eight, with a college degree in merchandising and marketing. She had come to Bridge's after serving as an assistant buyer for one of New York City's largest stores and has made a place for herself in this northwestern area in a very short time. Her assistant is Joy Maxwell, a recent "graduate" of the Bridge's Executive Training Squad. Both girls get along splendidly and make an excellent team as indicated by the department's profitable status. In fact, the Misses Dress Department's profit picture is held up as a model to other buyers by their respective divisional merchandise managers.

Bridge's is a full-service department store and as a result, the Misses Dress Department has a full complement of ten full-time salespeople, six part-time salespeople, two full-time stock people and three part-time stock people for Saturday and late openings. The Misses Dress Department enjoys practically a constant flow of good customer traffic all day long and a heavier flow on Saturdays. This keeps the sales force busy most of the time. These salespeople are mostly women who average about twenty years older than their buyer, and the average tenure of these salespeople is about fifteen years of loyal service to Bridge's. While they grudgingly admit that Matthews and Maxwell are "sharp cookies," these older women do not relish the idea of taking orders from women so much their junior. Both supervisors are keenly aware of the situation and they are generally very careful about giving the salespeople orders in order to keep them happy and still get the work done.

A trained observer, after a brief period in this department, could not help but notice the following:

1. Heavy customer traffic in the dress department engenders much stockwork, due to numerous and frequent try-ons.

61

2. The stock people frequently are unable to return tried on, unsold dresses to the floor stock because they are busy working with the assistant buyer on Returns-to-Vendors, branch store orders, markdowns, new merchandise, etc.
3. Dresses are being left in the dressing rooms by the customers and are being ignored by the salespeople who feel it is more important to sell. This causes loss of sales when both customers and salespeople cannot find wanted merchandise on the racks on the selling floor.
4. Salespeople frequently act as if stockwork is not part of their daily tasks and that it is beneath their professional standing.
5. Even when the assistant buyer tactfully requests assistance from salespeople in doing stockwork, the salespeople make a pretense of doing a little and then they find excuses or ways and means of avoiding the completion of the job.

Maxwell as assistant buyer is closer to the situation and finally finds it necessary to have a serious talk with Matthews since both the fall and holiday seasons are approaching, and things had to get worse. Matthews who has tried to delegate such responsibilities to her assistant and not get involved in such details agreed with Maxwell that the situation could get out of hand. She knows that as department head stockkeeping is one of her many responsibilities.

What should Cynthia Matthews, the buyer, do in this case?

Case 10
Is the Customer
Always Right?

Betty Griffen is a career salesperson in the Formal Dress Department of Harrington's, one of New York City's finest Fifth Avenue large specialty stores. Griffen has been employed at Harrington's for over fifteen years, coming to New York City from Chicago after her husband died to be near her daughter. She is a model employee and a fine salesperson who has built an enviable following at Harrington's. Her customers appreciate Betty's fine manner, merchandise knowledge, and service.

No one appreciates Betty Griffen more than Marian Thurm, the formal dress department buyer at Harrington's, who often wished she had a whole sales force made up of Betty Griffens.

On this particular day, one of Griffen's regular customers, Mrs. Leroy Stephensen III, came into the department with her teen-age daughter, Amanda. After exchanging greetings, Mrs. Stephensen told Griffen that Amanda had just received the much-coveted invitation to the Annual Sub-Debutante Cotillion sponsored by the snobbish New York Women's Art League.

While Amanda was not approaching marriageable age, Mrs. Stephensen confided, "This was a splendid chance to meet the boys of New York's best families."

As luck would have it, Mrs. Stephenensen spotted a gown for Amanda in ". . . just the right style and color for my little girl."

Luck ran out, however, when Griffen discovered that the only dress available in Amanda's size was damaged and was hanging on the door of Marian Thurm's office.

Thurm, as typical in most specialty stores, is not only the buyer but the department manager as well. She has the primary responsibility therefore for the department's sales activities as well as the buying and merchandising functions. As part of this responsibility, she has laid down a rule that a customer may be permitted to try on a damaged garment if it would help to determine size or color preference, but that no one in the department would ever be permitted to sell a damaged garment. It was her firm belief that in the long run, all such garments must be returned to the manufacturer for credit.

In addition, Thurm has trained her staff to seek her permission before even showing a damaged dress to a customer, which Betty Griffen had done.

Accordingly, this formal gown, which incidentally was priced at $195, a big ticket item, was only shown to Amanda because Betty felt that she could obtain a special order on it from the manufacturer.

After Amanda tried on the dress, her mother proclaimed, "Mandy, it's perfect . . . it's you!"

Griffen called the branch store assistant buyer who in turn not only checked her records but also called two of Harrington's branches that might have the dress, but with no success.

Griffen then offered to take a special order for her customer, having checked out this possibility with the buyer when she originally asked permission to show the damaged dress.

"Not on your life, my dear," said the dowager Mrs. Stephensen. "George, my husband, and I are leaving shortly for Carlsbad to take the waters. George has the gout, you know. I want to be sure that Amanda is all set for the ball. No, my dear, we'll take this dress and cover the damage on the shoulder with a corsage or a piece of jewelry."

Betty Griffen politely pointed out that department regulations prohibited her from selling the dress. Mrs. Stephensen then imperiously called for the department head.

Thurm was equally polite, but firm. "It's for your protection too, Madam. This dress is already charged back to the manufacturer and will be returned this afternoon. Please be assured that we will send you one in perfect condition, in plenty of time. . . ."

Mrs. Stephensen rose to her full height and said, "My dear, I want this dress for Amanda and not any special order that may never arrive. This ball is very important to my little girl's career. Mrs. Thomas Harrington and I play bridge every Thursday and I assure you I will go straight to Mr. Harrington's office from here. Now, pack that dress and charge it to my account. . . ."

If you were Marian Thurm, what would you do?

Case 11
The Old Guard
Never Retreats

Students of buying and merchandising and retailing know that "The Mazur Plan" promulgated by the National Retail Merchants Association (NRMA) in the late 1920's had a profound effect on the organizational structure of large American department and specialty stores. For the first time, in most specialty stores, lines of authority and responsibility were established; specialization became possible; and order replaced semi-chaos insofar as the store's table of organization was concerned.

There was only one apparent flaw in "The Mazur Plan." The failure to provide for a flow of responsibility of the entire merchandising/management function. This was clearly seen by the plan's proposal to give the supervision and control of the salespeople to both the Merchandising and Operations Divisions. Some three decades later, the NRMA proposed a new organization plan which was intended to supplant the Mazur Plan's *line* organization with a *line* and *staff* organization. Briefly, this new table of organization removed the selling function from the buyer and turned it over to a sales manager. The buyer's duties as outlined by this new plan were confined to planning, buying, and merchandising.[1]

Among the many large retail stores that switched with their own variations to the new line and staff plan was Hollander's. Hollander's was a department store located in New York City with branches in nine suburban areas. Because the greatest part of the company's sales volume came from fashion merchandise, Hollander's top management's interpretation of the new organizational plan resulted in removing all the buyers from their central city store location and providing them with large and palatial "buying office" space in a well-known Seventh Avenue showroom building in the heart of New York City's garment district. From this location, the buyers could practically walk to all their resources most of the time.

When the revamping of responsibilities was completed, Howard Apfelbaum was promoted from the trainee/head-of-stock position he had held for almost a year to the new job title of sales manager

---

1. For complete information, please see: Sidney Packard, Arthur A. Winters, Nathan Axelrod, *Fashion Buying and Merchandising*, New York: Fairchild Publications, 1976, pp. 47–56.

of the Men's Sportswear Department at Hollander's main store in midtown New York. Howard had been graduated from one of the City University of New York's community colleges in his native Brooklyn and had been recruited by Hollander's to join their On-the-Job Training Program. He found the hours long, the work arduous, but the challenge stimulating. Of course, he was very pleased with his new job and the pay increase it provided.

Dan Pasternack, the men's sportswear buyer, had been with Hollander's for more than forty-five years. He had started as a stock boy during the early days of the Great Depression and as the store grew, he, too, advanced, albeit very slowly as compared to modern times. Of course, Pasternack was terribly upset and much displeased by the new turn of events that removed him from the selling floor and ensconced him in a big, new office on Seventh Avenue. He was now one of a few of the "Old Guard" left in the store; and in the opinion of the new top management that Stanley Hollander, the founder's son, had brought into the office, "a neanderthal anachronism."

Thus, it was no surprise to those observers of the scene that Dan Pasternack frequently chose to ignore the new table of organization that now limited his duties in the Men's Sportswear Department. It was easy for him to visit the large midtown Hollander Store and interfere with the running of the department by shifting merchandise around and by giving the salespeople orders that conflicted with the tasks assigned to them by Howard Apfelbaum. Howard, who had a great respect for buyers in general, kept his tongue and when Pasternack left, he merely countermanded the orders and let it go at that.

On this particular day, however, things were different. Howard came back from lunch to find the department crowded with customers as a result of a big ad in the New York *Daily News;* but the salespeople were busy switching the location of the department's large stock of sport jackets.

He discovered that while he was out Pasternack had come by and ordered the change—a task and responsibility that was no longer his. Howard immediately dispatched the salespeople to wait on trade and he personally returned the sport jackets to their regular location.

Now, however, despite his seeming lack of executive experience and his permissiveness in his dealings with Pasternack, Howard realized that he had to take steps to assert his own authority before it was too late.

If you were in Howard Apfelbaum's place, what would you do?

Case 12
The General
Merchandise Manager
has a Problem

The Colonial Department Store had an Executive Training Program that combined the best of the several types of programs commonly used by stores of similar size and structure. It consisted of mornings being devoted to regular classes much like a college. Here the staff members of the Executive Development Department taught thirty carefully selected executive trainees courses such as Merchandising Mathematics, Principles of Sales Promotion, Supervisory Techniques, Sales Training Practices. In addition, there was a regularly scheduled group of lectures, seminars, and workshops conducted by the heads of the various divisions and departments of the store, e.g., the Controller, the Protection Manager.

In the second phase of this training program, the trainees work part-time during the afternoons and full-time in busy selling seasons, in various non-selling and selling departments. They were on a computerized schedule that gave the Training Department instant information if they wished to locate the trainee. The length of the trainees stay in each of these areas depended on the time of the year as well as the nature of the department. This job rotation phase gave both the trainee and the store's management people an opportunity to look each other over for future placement possibilities. In toto, this training program lasted an average of twelve months. It was a common practice for a buyer or other department head, when a junior executive vacancy occurred under their supervision, to request that an executive trainee from the squad be detached for a "permanent placement" appointment.

Barbara Murray, the divisional merchandise manager of children's wear at Colonial, was a guest speaker at a Career Day Conference at a local college and she explained Colonial's Training Program to a large group of interested seniors, among whom the most intent was Roberta Parker.

Roberta, an attractive, vivacious, alert and charming young woman asked many intelligent questions and showed so much enthusiasm for the presentation that Murray invited her to have lunch with her at Colonial the next day. Things went so well between them that

Murray arranged an interview with Jack Price, the manager of Executive Development.

Thus, with the strong backing of Murray, and after testing and in-depth interviewing, Price offered Roberta a place on Colonial's Training Squad when she graduated in June. In the meantime, Murray persuaded Roberta to take a Thursday-evening-Saturday-extra selling job in the Infant's Wear Department so that they could "stay in touch."

Needless to say, Roberta Parker was walking on "Cloud Nine." Her future seemed assured. After a brief, post-graduation vacation, she took her place in the various classes of Colonial's Training Program and was also assigned to a job rotation schedule. She made it her business, however, to keep in contact with Murray, although her class and work schedule kept her very busy. Unbeknownst to Roberta, Murray was also keeping tabs on her because she now regarded her as her protégée.

About a year later, an assistant buyer's position became vacant in the Girl's Dress Department and Murray, using her considerable influence, secured Roberta's release from the Training Squad and had the promotion arranged for her. Of course, Roberta was thrilled by the prospect of becoming a junior executive so soon and she was the envy of the rest of the executive trainees.

Roberta plunged right in to learning the department—its resources, stock, salespeople, etc. With her accustomed vitality and enthusiasm, she was soon doing a great job. Murray kept close watch on her progress and frequently checked with Olga Gordon, the Girls' Dress Department buyer. Things went along smoothly and Roberta continued to earn the approbation of her supervisors.

However, after about a year and a half as assistant buyer in the Girls' Dress Department, Roberta became restless and somewhat bored. She felt she was stalled and stymied, with very little to learn, few challenges to meet and no further advancement in the children's wear division apparent. She yearned for more action, a bigger job, and more remuneration. She thought of speaking to Murray but hesitated. Among other things she felt that she might seem to be ungrateful if she asked for an opportunity to advance in other areas of the Colonial Department Store.

Instead, when Murray and Gordon were away on an extended market trip, she asked Price to arrange an appointment for her with Peter Chamberlain, Colonial's corporate personnel director. Chamberlain, a highly professional personnel manager, before seeing Roberta, made an intensive study of her personnel file and ratings. He had also made a few discreet phone calls around the store and had spoken at length to Price, the Executive Development Manager, who reported to him. This was all in anticipation of what Roberta had on her mind because when Jack Price had requested the appointment, he indicated that Roberta wanted "to discuss her future at Colonial."

At the appointed day and hour, Roberta appeared at Chamberlain's office and he soon put her at ease. He quickly found her to measure up to all the reports and records and then some. Roberta told Chamberlain that while there was no apparent urgency, she felt she was in a dead end in her division and she believed she was capable of handling bigger and better things anywhere in the store. She indicated she was not fussy about the department or division as long as the opportunity for promotion existed. She also gave Chamberlain to understand that if he were unable to help her achieve her goal, she would reluctantly have to look elsewhere, even if it meant relocating. Chamberlain hastened to assure her of his wholehearted understanding and he promised to cooperate to the fullest extent. She requested and he readily agreed to keep their conversation confidential.

Chamberlain was well aware of Roberta Parker's value to Colonial and he informed her of his efforts on her behalf from time to time during the months that followed. One day, Hartley Davidson, the divisional merchandise manager who supervised the various coat departments, called on Price and told him that he had just received approval from William Knight, the general merchandise manager, to create a new position in the Better Coat Department for an associate buyership, with market responsibility for sport coats.

He asked Price to prepare recommendations for candidates to fill this new job from either inside or outside the store. Before Price could raise the question, Davidson bluntly informed him that he had no assistant buyer in his own division that he felt he could accept, or even recommend. In fact, he felt that he wanted fresh blood—someone with imagination, enthusiasm, and initiative.

In a flash, Price thought of Roberta Parker and said, "Mr. Davidson, I have somebody for you in the store and I guarantee that in less than five minutes after you meet Roberta Parker she will be your new associate buyer."

He thereupon got Roberta's file and gave Davidson a thorough briefing on her. Davidson agreed that her record was exemplary and that her personal profile as sketched by Price seemed to fit the bill.

"You know," Davidson said, "I belong to that school of merchandise administrators who believe that to be a *merchant* is more important than the momentary gain of securing someone who has direct product or merchandise information experience. I worked for Macy's before I came here and the candy buyer was promoted to head the Drapery and Bedspread Department because it was evident that he knew how to *merchandise* his department. In a few weeks, a buyer can become proficient and in less than six months, expert in selecting market resources. And evidently this kid has it!"

However, Davidson pointed out, "Mr. Price, you know that we have an unwritten law here at Colonial to prevent 'raiding.' I'm not permitted to interview Ms. Parker unless I have Barbara Murray's permission. So you better clear it with her as soon as you can."

When Price approached Murray and gave her the background, he was a little startled by the storm that was unleashed.

"Listen, Price," Murray fumed, "you keep your hands off Roberta. She's my protégée—I recruited her from school; got her on the squad; handpicked her for my division and there she stays. I didn't train her for that Davidson guy or anyone else to pick off. It's true that I don't see any promotion possibilities in the children's wear division for the forseeable future, but she's young yet. . . ."

In vain, Price tried to point out that the girl was an asset to the store; that she would be lost to Colonial and go elsewhere; and that it was unfair to Roberta, the Coat Department, and the store to hold her back.

"Look, Roberta owes me," replied Murray. "I'll handle her, don't worry. Now, bug off."

Price reported his lack of success to Hartley Davidson. By this time, Davidson had checked on his own and Roberta seemed to be made to order for the new job. Davidson felt that Murray was completely wrong in this matter, and that it was up to the general merchandise manager to settle the problem at this point.

If you were William Knight, the general merchandise manager, how would you handle the matter?

VI

THE FASHION BUYER'S RESPONSIBILITIES IN A LARGE RETAIL STORE

A buyer is a merchandising executive who has as one of his major responsibilities the task of picking and maintaining a stock of the proper merchandise for the store's customers.

It should be quite obvious that the type and size of the organization will make a great deal of difference to the buyer's responsibility. The authors have elected to analyze the buyer's responsibilities in a large retail store for two reasons: (1) this is the area where there are more buyers than any other in the fashion buying and merchandising field; and (2) a large store requires the greatest number of responsibilities and provides the opportunity to analyze the subject from the widest viewpoint.

The following is a brief list of the important and most frequently found buyer's responsibilities. How many of these responsibilities are assigned to the buyer depends on the practice of the store. Variations are too numerous for a less than extended explanation.

1. *Planning*
   A. Assist in the preparation, or development, of the Six

Month Buying Plan and activities related to the department's merchandise budget.

B. Plan inventories in accordance with the policies established by management.

C. Work with the divisional merchandise manager on revising merchandise plans.

2. *Buying*

A. Purchase merchandise in accordance with approved buying plans and Open-to-Buy.

B. Maintain a balanced stock of merchandise wanted by the store's customers at the right price.

C. Establish and maintain effective buying relationships with approved merchandise resources.

D. Determine not only *what* and *when* to buy, but also *where* and *how much* to spend.

E. The actual purchasing process involving all steps up to placing the actual order; follow-up on order.

F. Organize the trip to the market, including the work of the resident buying office.

3. *Pricing and Profits*

A. Secure the best possible markup, price changes including markdowns.

B. Stock the department's price lines and price zones in line with the store's policies.

C. Keep accurate records of both the book and the physical inventories.

D. Protect the merchandise from all kinds of loss.

4. *Selling*

A. Despite some movement in the direction of separating buying from selling, most buyers are still in charge of the sales activities of the department.

B. Give salespeople merchandise information, either informally or by means of department meetings.

C. Provide adequate customer coverage.

D. Obtain sales promotion aids from vendors.

5. *Sales Promotion*

A. Plan and supervise department displays.

B. Be alert for items that lend themselves to sales promotion campaigns.

C. Select merchandise for advertising and give advertising department adequate information for the advertisement.

D. Once merchandise is advertised for sale, insure that

the merchandise is on hand; inform salespeople; record and evaluate response to the advertisement.

6. *The Resident Buying Office*

The work of the resident buying office will be discussed in Chapter VIII. This reference is merely to indicate that the buyer has a responsibility and a relationship to the store's buying office which acts as its market representative.

7. *Branch Stores*

In many instances, throughout the country, branch stores have become more important than the main store, which is often located in a declining, downtown shopping district.

A. The buyer needs to analyze how each branch and its merchandise needs differs not only from the main store, but also from each other.

B. There is a need for the best possible main store—branch store buyer communication setup.

C. The buyer should have a clear view of such branch store merchandising precepts as sales of basic stock items; merchandise backup of advertised items; slow sellers; markdowns.

8. *Inventory Shortages*

One of the buyer's most troublesome responsibilities is that arising from inventory shortages, the cause of which are frequently out of buyer control. It should be noted that many firms use an increase or decrease in the department's inventory shortages as an important part in appraising the buyer's worth to the store. Accordingly, the buyer must exercise constant vigilance in supervising the clerical or recordkeeping work of the department; be aware of the sloppiness of salespeople in handling the pricing of merchandise with lost sales tags; be careful of the procedures used in the regularly scheduled department physical inventories; and be aware that proper placement of stock on the selling floor can discourage pilferage.

9. *Vendor Relations*

It has been said that a buyer is frequently as good as his merchandise resources. While it is probably true that some vendors come and go, the principal sources of merchandise are usually the ones who have had a long and profitable relationship with the store. Good buyers adhere to the following, well-established principles of good vendor relations:

    A. There should be a mutually held belief that both the store and the vendor need each other for success.

    B. The buyer should always honor appointments with vendors.

    C. Resources should be sought, developed, and cultivated for such a period of time as they are mutually profitable.

    D. The buyer should be fair in the matter of merchandise returns.

10. *Foreign Buying*

Foreign buying will be covered in Chapter XIII, but it is our purpose here to indicate that vast quantities of imported merchandise are being offered for sale. Thus, the buyer's responsibility for securing merchandise takes on a new and frequently difficult challenge to his ability.

11. *Brands*

Many buyers in fashion merchandise rely heavily on the use of nationally branded merchandise because they feel that brands are more readily accepted by customers. Some stores develop private or store brands, which depend primarily on the store's reputation. It is the buyer's responsibility to study the sales performance of the branded merchandise in his department and to develop an understanding of its use.

12. *Receiving and Marking*

    A. Purchase order data on file with marking and receiving areas is correct.

    B. Insure that merchandise is as ordered.

    C. Give marking room all the information needed for price tags.

    D. Give marking room a distribution plan which includes shipment to branches, or storage in stockrooms, or delivery to floor.

    E. Authorize payment of invoice after merchandise is received and checked.

13. *Traffic*

    A. Since the buyer must add the cost of transporting goods from the vendor to the store, the buyer is thus responsible to provide specific instructions on how to ship these goods.

    B. The buyer should also realize and understand the costs

of frequent, small deliveries, and ship merchandise the fastest way.

14. *Personnel*

The buyer's personnel responsibilities are twofold: the rank-and-file department personnel and selecting and training those junior executives who assist in the buying and merchandising processes. These personnel responsibilities may be delineated into the following major categories:

A. Training *all* department personnel in such areas as policies, selling techniques, merchandise and sales promotion information, systems and procedures, rules and regulations.

B. Communicating on various levels such as human relations, supervision; and most importantly communicating enthusiasm for the merchandise purchased that must be sold by others.

C. Delegating many parts of the responsibilities outlined in this entire section to both subordinates and assistants. In delegating all or part of the responsibilities, the buyer must be aware of the importance of selecting the right person and to give that person not only the *responsibility* for the work involved, but also the *authority* needed to do so. The buyer must follow-up such delegation.

15. *Government Regulations*

The fashion buyer is confronted daily with legal responsibilities arising primarily from Federal laws regulating fabric content, merchandise claims in advertising, and in making buying arrangements with vendors, particularly with reference to prices. In brief, the buyer must be aware of the certain legal areas in his regular merchandising activities such as the Robinson-Patman Act, the Wool Products Labeling Act, the Textile Fiber Products Identification Act.

16. *Stockkeeping*

A. Maintain a constant flow of merchandise from the receiving and marking rooms to the department's selling floor or stockrooms.

B. Assure that the merchandise is arranged so that it is not only attractive but also convenient for the customer to inspect and handle.

C. Arrange related items for easier selling.

D. Keep stock clean, properly folded or hung, and protected from soiling.

17. *Housekeeping**

It is quite understandable why housekeeping might be confused with stockkeeping (see above). Stockkeeping duties are primarily concerned with a well-arranged and a well-kept stock. Good housekeeping, however, goes beyond good merchandise arrangements and includes such buyer responsibilities as:

A. Neat, clean and uncluttered dressing rooms.

B. Clean, sparkling counter tops and showcases.

C. Clean, neat, well-coordinated merchandise displays.

D. Flat merchandise folded; hanging merchandise buttoned, zippered, belted, and centered on hangers.

E. Signs that are clean and clearly stated.

18. *Credit***

The buyer must have a knowledge and an understanding of the use of credit by the store's customers, since it is a fundamental concept of American economics that retail credit, which gives the customer immediate possession and use of merchandise, is a way of life. The buyer's knowledge of the store's credit operation must be thorough so that he can communicate this information to his salespeople.

19. *Supervision*

Supervising people comes with the job, since the buyer is also a department head. Supervising entails, in the simplest sense, *getting work done through people.* In the complex job of supervision, the buyer must be tactful, patient, decisive, realistic, fair, and able to plan and organize all the department's activities.

---

* In most larger stores, this task is the responsibility of operations, but from the broadest aspect, the buyer as a department manager can demand and influence appropriate personnel to maintain high standards of housekeeping.

** An administrative function in which a buyer has a peripheral influence, if any.

Case 13
The Price Change

Lillian Shore is the hosiery buyer for Marshall's Department Store, a very large retailing establishment located in the largest city in the Southwest. Marshall's merchandising policies emphasize the sale of nationally branded merchandise. The store has won many prizes in the past awarded by the National Brand Foundation. While the Hosiery Department carries its own "Marshall Mills Brand," it relies most heavily on national brands such as Hanes, Fruit of the Loom, Kayser-Roth.

Shore has recently completed negotiations for a very large order representing over 20% of her stock with Atlantic Mills, owners of one of the national brands, for her regular stock as well as for several special promotions.

In addition to the special prices obtained by Shore, she was also able to lower her costs by persuading the manufacturer to ship early so that she could take anticipation as well as the regular discount. All in all, she was satisfied that she had obtained the hosiery at the best possible, rock-bottom prices from Theodore Eaton, the sales manager for Atlantic Mills.

Shortly thereafter, on arriving at the store one day, Shore found a number of "urgent" telephone messages on her desk from another important nationally branded hosiery manufacturer, Van Buren Mills. When she returned the calls, she discovered from Sam Baker, the sales manager, that Van Buren Mills had decided to drop their hosiery prices by a flat 7½% in order to stimulate business in this highly competitive field. This news spread like wildfire throughout the hosiery market and it soon became evident that the other important hosiery mills would probably have to follow suit in order to meet the competition.

It did not take Shore too long to put in a call to Eaton at Atlantic Mills.

"Say Ted," she began, "I guess you know why I'm calling. The Van Buren Mills price cut is all over the market and you must be on a hot spot."

"Lil," said Eaton, "I'm surprised that you should call me about that. I swear that I gave you a rock-bottom price and including the other discounts, you're way ahead of the game. It seems to me that you're being unfair asking for an additional price decrease."

Eaton had worked with Lillian Shore for many years and they

had gotten along very well. However, Shore insisted on a price adjustment and threatened to cancel the large order with Atlantic Mills and place it with Van Buren Mills.

How do you view Lillian Shore's actions?

Case 14
Restraint of Trade?

The Superior Department Store is located in a metropolitan city in New England and prides itself on the better merchandise it carries for an affluent clientele. While the store's name indicates the full line of merchandise that makes it worthy of the name "department store," it is a specialty department store with the emphasis on fashion merchandise. Like many specialty stores, there is at least one outstanding merchandising area for which it is widely known—in this case, the dress departments. Oscar Shepherd is the divisional merchandise manager of the dress division and has been with The Superior for over twenty-five years. Sybil Duncan is the buyer of women's dresses and is highly regarded.

One of the Women's Dress Department's key resources is the Dixie Dress Company, with showrooms in New York City, Atlanta, and Los Angeles and a modern, magnificent manufacturing facility in Flatrock, North Carolina. Sybil Duncan brought the Dixie Dress line with her when she came to Superior from her last position in the Midwest. She has close ties to Dixie Dress and its sales manager, Garrett Evans, because they were both from the same town in Georgia. Duncan felt that Dixie Dress shipped a very well-made garment that was styled particularly fine for the larger, matronly woman. Evans had agreed at the beginning of the relationship with Superior that Duncan's department would be the exclusive distributors for Dixie Dress in the trading area. In return for this exclusivity, The Superior invested a great deal of their advertising space and money over the three years that the line had been featured. Sales, also, had come along splendidly once their New England customers began to appreciate the fine fabrics, good design, and excellent finishing details of Dixie dresses. Duncan's annual volume with Dixie had increased to well over five thousand dresses with an average cost of $39.75 which meant over $300,000 at retail for Dixie Dress. As a result, this company now accounted for a sizable portion of the Women's Dress Department's volume.

This ideal arrangement came to a grinding halt one day when Ike Plunkett, the "road man," for Dixie Dresses called from a nearby New England city and asked to meet with Oscar Shepherd and Sybil Duncan. Actually, Garrett Evans should have called for this meeting, but his personal ties to Sybil Duncan embarrassed this courtly southern gentleman. Hence, Plunkett drew the "dirty work" assignment.

79

In essence, Plunkett brought this message from the Dixie Dress management:

- They needed more sales volume. The firm was in an expansion cycle and they were looking for more outlets for their merchandise.
- They were thus approaching stores they had refused to sell before, because of their previous policy of granting exclusivity to the best store in town.

In The Superior's area, Woodward's Department Store has long sought to buy some of Dixie's lower priced lines but had never succeeded. Woodward's was a full-fledged department store with highly promotional merchandising policies. At times, their ads give the impression that they are a discount organization. While The Superior's emphasis is on quality and service, Woodward's image, as reflected by their ads and other communications, shouts "PRICE."

Oscar Shepherd was livid.

"You mean to tell me that after all this time, effort, and money, you want us to share your merchandise with that 'Cheap Charlie' store?"

Uncomfortably, Ike Plunkett pointed out: "Mr. Shepherd, we have definite assurances that with their overall sales volume, we can more than double our sales in this city."

"Do you know what this will do to Superior's customers?" Sybil Duncan asked. "She would see her maid, or at best, her husband's bookkeeper coming and going in her own dresses."

Plunkett hastened to assure her that this could not happen because each store would have exclusive rights to certain styles which would be confined to that store. In addition, there would be less chance of conflict since Woodward's price zones would confine their buyers to those numbers which Superior never bought anyway.

"Have you ever seen Woodward's ads?" queried Shepherd. "They yell PRICE, PRICE, PRICE and they frequently cut prices at the slightest pretext. With a nationally known name like Dixie Dress, they will make a football out of your merchandise."

Both Oscar Shepherd and Sybil Duncan continued to argue, plead, and cajole, but it soon became apparent that Ike Plunkett was only a "messenger" who was there to carry out orders from Garrett Evans.

What should The Superior Department Store do?

Case 15
A Retail Tug of War

S & L Dresses, Inc. has been one of the largest and most successful junior dress firms since the inception of the junior-sized category. They were particularly an important resource with Newman's Department Store which was located in New York City and where the S & L line accounted for about 30% of the Junior Dress Department's annual sales volume. This situation was repeated in department and specialty stores all over the United States.

As a result of an in-depth marketing research study prepared for S & L Dresses by one of the nation's largest consulting firms, the company decided to switch from the junior to the missy-sized customer segment. Hard-nosed information pointed to the fact that there were many more missy-sized women with more money to spend than there were junior-sized women. The survey also revealed that the junior-sized customer was not so dress conscious any more. Although S & L Dresses had done very well with the junior-sized customer, they reluctantly agreed that a progressive organization must always look ahead to new markets when it becomes necessary or apparent.

In view of their large sales volume, and because they were good friends, Joseph Solomon, president of S & L Dresses personally called Norbert Barnett, president of Newman's Department Store, and informed him that effective with the new fall season, the S & L line would not be shown to the junior dress buyers but would only be available in the missy sizes. Of course, Barnett was surprised, but he understood the reasoning behind the decision after Solomon's explanation.

Accordingly, Barnett passed the word down the chain of command until Jeri Middleton, the junior dress buyer, received the bad news. Of course, she was beside herself at this sudden turn of events. She envied the missy dress buyer's new good fortune, but like the good soldier that she was, she went about replacing the more than 30% of her sales volume that the S & L line represented by cultivating and developing other junior dress resources that she had neglected up to now. The S & L fall merchandise was eventually delivered to the Missy Department, since it was top management's decision to continue to buy the line for Newman's with which it had long been identified.

After the fall season was over, S & L's principals did an abrupt about-face and re-entered the junior dress business. They had found competition from established missy-sized firms greater than they had anticipated. Their merchandise did not sell as well as expected, and their "touch" was better for juniors than for misses. They were a bit too perky, too cute, too young for the missy market—smart for juniors but not for misses.

S & L Dresses began to contact all the big stores and attempted to recapture their former place in the junior market. They had no problem in handling the independent specialty stores because these individual owners can decide where to put the merchandise and can mix merchandise and classify it more freely. In department stores, it was different. Departments are frequently structured by size classification, for example, and thus there are different departments and different buyers.

James O'Keefe, the ready-to-wear merchandise manager of Newman's called Middleton, the junior dress buyer, and said, "I have great news for you, Jeri—you're getting the S & L line back as your prime resource. They're going to be making junior dresses again."

Middleton shuddered at the news. During the past season, she reminded her boss, she had replaced the S & L dress line with several other resources and her figures were well ahead of the previous fall.

"I'll be up to see you in five minutes—don't go away," Middleton begged.

She had no sooner seated herself at O'Keefe's desk when she began, "My stock turnover is better now because I'm in a position to shop the market with a greater amount of open-to-buy since I'm not tied up with the huge commitment that S & L demanded every season. I'm doing a better job than ever before . . . so they can keep the line . . . I don't need it . . . I don't want it. . . ."

The divisional merchandise manager pointed out that the store had spent a great deal of time, effort, and money building up the S & L merchandise.

"If the S & L dresses are not in any department in our store," O'Keefe said, "all that effort and investment Newman's has made will be passed on to Blair's Department Store across the street—and you know how long they've been aching to get that merchandise."

Jeri Middleton continued to remonstrate with her boss, offering to prove conclusively by her records that the Junior Dress Department was much better off now and would continue to be in the future.

"My stock looks better," she said. "My maintained markup is better . . . I can change things more often. . . ."

The merchandise manager pointed out, finally, that brand

decisions of this magnitude are management's decision.

"A key resource such as S & L helps to build the character of the department. We must think this over very carefully and believe me, it is not an easy decision to make."

If you were Jeri Middleton, the buyer, how would you proceed?

Case 16
The Power of
the Pencil

Guido Paolluci Knitwear Company is a very successful manufacturer of medium to better double knit garments. They feature
knits with jacquard design motifs which are woven on Italian knitting
machines in the United States. The two principals of the firm are
Irving Copeland, who is "inside" handling production, purchasing,
etc. and Bill Samuels, who is "outside" taking charge of marketing
and sales functions. The firm's merchandise is well known in its field
as a result of years of regular advertising in a variety of fashion
magazines as well as in repeated store (co-op) ads. The company has
also received a "good press" from the excellent work of its public
relations agency. Guido, as it is frequently called, is sold in many
large department and specialty stores and in hundreds of better
independent stores thoughout the country. They have over two
thousand accounts and a sales volume approaching $5 million per
annum.

Meryl Alexander is the buyer for Benson's Department Store,
a prestigious retailer in a large West Coast metropolis. Alexander
came to Benson's from a fine specialty store in the Midwest because
her husband had been transferred to his firm's new offices near Benson's main store. Benson's felt extremely fortunate to get someone
like Meryl Alexander who was known in her market as a fashion
innovator as well as a good promotion authority.

On one of her early buying trips to New York, Alexander went
to the Guido Paolluci showroom and had a reunion with Bill Samuels.
After exchanging hearty greetings and nostalgic reminiscences,
Alexander got down to business and went over the line with Samuels.

Benson's in addition to its main store had nine branches in the
surrounding suburban areas. Many of the branch stores were in upper-middle class sections of the metropolitan area.

Guido had never sold Benson's before but Alexander, an old
customer of theirs, knew the firm well and had done an excellent job
with their merchandise in the past.

When she had reviewed the line, Alexander turned to Samuels
and asked a simple question: "Bill, who do you sell to in my area? And

who do you intend to sell in the immediate future?"*

In reply to her question, Bill Samuels told Meryl Alexander that there were six independent stores in her area that were currently carrying the Guido line.

Alexander indicated that her opening order for Benson's and its branches would be much greater than those six stores total annual purchases combined; and, of course, there was the undeniable prospect of sizable reorders.

Overcome by the probable size of the forthcoming Benson business, Bill Samuels rapidly lost his sense of loyalty to the six independent stores. Bill Samuels, doing some rapid mental arithmetic, came to an understanding that Benson's with its branches probably would use about two thousand pieces for the season whereas the six smaller stores would each wind up with an average of sixty to one hundred pieces for the same period. Although Samuels would like to continue to sell the six independent stores as well, he knew that he could not have his cake and eat it, too.

He and Alexander agreed that he could not cancel the independent stores' orders because this would be a direct violation of Federal anti-trust statutes and it was still fresh in his memory that three of the most prestigious fashion stores in the country had recently been found guilty of just such a violation. Accordingly, he agreed to kick their orders around until they got lost for the current season and in the future, he would dream up further measures designed to discourage the local stores from ordering the Guido line.

Soon after, the merchandise began to arrive at Benson's and as expected, it did very well. About this time, Jerry Peters, owner of Peter's Fashions, Inc. and Harold Tillman, of Milady's, Ltd., accidentally met in the bar at Rudi's, a well-known eating establishment.

---

* Meryl Alexander's question was a natural one. As a generic group, large retail organizations frequently seek, as individuals, to control the distribution policies of manufacturers. This is in exchange for the opportunity granted by the large store when it places an order—usually a good size one—that permits the manufacturer to use the order to influence other stores in purchasing its line. When a well-known store places an order and advertises his product, the manufacturer and his sales force can use the order and the ads to help other buyers overcome the basic insecurity involved in the buying of fashion goods. Thus, when a buyer sees that a major store(s) has made a buying decision in a particular category or classification, that buyer thinks that what is good enough for Marshall Field.... Then again, there is also another reason for the large store to attempt to control the manufacturer's distribution, since it will lead to the possibility of eliminating as much competition as possible, it helps to get the jump in their entire trading area; and it gives them the leadership that is so helpful, particularly with the well-known, nationally branded merchandise.

Being friendly non-competitors (Peter's Fashions was located in a nearby suburb, while Milady's was a downtown competitor of Benson's main store), they had a drink together and decided to dine together.

During the course of the meal, Tillman asked Peters how business was and particularly how the new Guido Paolluci merchandise was moving.

"How could I know? I never received one piece of it," Peters replied.

"Son of a gun, neither did I," mused Tillman. "I wonder what's going on."

"Hey, wait a minute, Hal," said Jerry Peters, "Did you see that Benson ad on the Guido merchandise? I'll bet that's the answer—they're trying to freeze us little guys out."

Before they parted company that evening, Harold Tillman and Jerry Peters, to avoid any semblance of collusion, decided to begin simultaneous but independent action to rescue their Guido merchandise orders. They agreed to call Bill Samuels at separate intervals and if they received no satisfaction, to have their attorneys threaten him with civil as well as criminal action. They also agreed to check the other four independent stores and see if they were in the same boat.

When Jerry Peters reached Bill Samuels in New York, he accused Guido of giving Benson's preferential treatment, which, of course, Samuels denied. Samuels professed ignorance of the order and said he would look into the matter. Jerry Peters then reported this conversation to Harold Tillman.

Another call to New York brought a similar response, ignorance of the order and the promise of investigation. Both men agreed that there must be collusion between Benson's and Guido's and now was the time for action.

If you were advising Jerry Peters and Harold Tillman, how would you go about handling this situation?

VII

FASHION BUYING FOR CENTRAL CHAIN AND MAIL-ORDER ORGANIZATIONS

THE CHAIN

A *chain* is usually defined as a group of four or more stores (although some marketing authorities also use the figures two or three or more stores) that are centrally owned, managed, and merchandised.* In addition to these characteristics, chains are usually also known for their separation of the buying selling functions; the use of highly specialized personnel; the tendency towards standardization in merchandising, layout, fixtures, etc.; and by their huge purchasing power which engenders quantity discounts and therefore lower wholesale prices.

Chains may be classified in a number of ways:

1. By ownership—corporate chains, franchise chains, leased department chains, voluntary chains, and manufacturers' chains.
2. By geography—multi-national chains, national chains, regional chains, metropolitan area chains, and local chains.
3. By fashion merchandise categories—shoe chains, men's wear chains, specialty store chains, infant's and children's wear chains, etc.

---

* Main office usually in the major market.

CENTRAL BUYING

One of the chain's chief characteristics is that it uses central buying and merchandising. There are three principal variations extant in the central buying and merchandising area.

THE CENTRAL MERCHANDISING PLAN

This plan involves keeping a tight control of the entire buying and merchandising process at the central office of the chain, with the store's function solely concerned with selling the merchandise. Despite its seeming advantages which include the employment of market specialists, volume buying which guarantees quantity discounts, lower prices, and frequently exclusivity, there are some definite limitations to this plan. These disadvantages include the problems that naturally arise from separating buying from selling, especially where great distances are concerned and the difficulty of merchandising by statistical records alone.

THE CENTRAL PURCHASE WITH MERCHANDISE-REQUISITION-PLAN

This plan attempts to overcome the limitations discussed in the central merchandise plan. The local store manager, or one of his department heads, is given the opportunity to control the amount and classifications of merchandise shipped to their store, particularly in the case of basic stock. The central buying office purchases large amounts of merchandise at good prices and warehouses them in a distribution center(s). Each store is able to requisition merchandise from stocklists prepared by the central buying office. This gives the local store manager an opportunity to select and requisition merchandise he feels can sell best and omit those items he has doubts about.

THE LISTING OR PRICE AGREEMENT PLAN

Under this plan, the store manager has the greatest autonomy in selecting merchandise for his store. The central buying office prepares catalogues wherein the merchandise is sketched, photographed and described. The central buyer makes definite commitments for these goods with chosen resources based on his best estimates and past sales. The manufacturer produces the merchandise, which is actually owned by the chain, and awaits orders from each store at the prices and other terms agreed upon by the central buyer. The store manager may or may not buy this merchandise but if he does, he does so in quantities, sizes, colors, etc, he deems best. If the merchandise is ordered, it is shipped directly to the store. The central buying office receives copies of each store order in order to be able to keep a running record of the inventory on hand at each of the manufacturers' premises.

THE MAIL-ORDER HOUSE

A mail-order house is a retail organization that seeks its business and its customers by means of catalogues or other printed media. It primarily uses the mails to both solicit and deliver the merchandise sold to its customers.

Mail-order houses usually fit into the following major classifications:

1. *General Merchandise Firms*—which offer a complete line of both hard and soft goods for sale through their catalogues.
2. *Specialized Merchandise Firms*—which offer a specialized, narrow line of goods such as fashion apparel, men's wear, shoes, books, records.
3. Mail-Order Departments of Large Stores*—most of the nation's larger department and specialty stores issue catalogues at various times of the year such as for "white" sales, the beginning of apparel seasons, back-to-school, Christmas. This is in addition to their daily newspaper ads which frequently solicit mail-order business.
4. *Advertising media mail-order firms*—using television, radio, national magazines, newspapers, etc. Many mail-order firms are in the business of selling merchandise by mail successfully.

To analyze the mail-order house as a contemporary fashion merchandising institution, a comparison of its advantages and disadvantages is quite interesting.

---

* Although they are conventional retailers, they are listed under mail-order organizations because of the growing importance and their market share of the mail-order business.

ADVANTAGES

1. It is convenient for a large sector of the public whose time is limited for personal shopping for any number of reasons, e.g., the working woman.
2. It saves the shopper money as well as time by avoiding traffic, parking hassles, costly gasoline consumption, etc.; and enables the shopper to select merchandise while enjoying all the comforts of home.
3. The shopping public has come to believe in the integrity of the merchandise offered because of the reputation enjoyed by the giants of the mail-order industry.
4. The breadth and depth of the merchandise offerings is frequently so great that customers do not feel at all restricted in their choice of goods.
5. The customers have come to know and believe that not only is the merchandise good quality at fair prices, but that it is frequently made to the mail-order houses' own specifications and under rigid quality control conditions which tend to assure them of satisfaction in advance.
6. The written guarantee of satisfaction is a normal aspect of mail-order selling and a liberal return policy adds to further customer gratification.
7. The firm may own or control many of its sources of supply (vertical integration) and this assures customers of good prices, quality merchandise and excellent delivery.

DISADVANTAGES

1. The cost of printing and distributing a sizable number of catalogues and supplements each year requires that each catalogue (and thus almost each item therein) brings in a better than adequate sales volume per issue.
2. Despite modern computers, mechanization, etc., getting the merchandise to the customer on time will always remain a problem. Customers are frequently impatient and can be annoyed at the delay between the time of mailing in the order and the receipt of the merchandise. (This time lag has been partially eliminated by the use of catalogue stores and catalogue counters within those retail chains that are in the mail-order business as well.)
3. Mail-order firms by virtue of the operation itself have the need to buy and stock large quantities of merchandise far

enough in advance of each selling season to have a good assortment of merchandise on hand for a much longer period of time than most stores. This could cause markdowns and create clearance merchandise.

It is obvious, with Sears, Roebuck as only one example, now doing more than $2 billion per annum in mail-order business alone, that the advantages outweigh the disadvantages and will probably continue to do so. Thus, it would seem that mail-order houses are not an anachronism but a flourishing factor in merchandise distribution.

Case 17
Sam, You Made the
Pants Too Short

Beacon's is a national mail-order firm with headquarters on the East Coast, which specializes in the sale of men's slacks and shoes. It does not issue catalogues but relies on periodic circulars to reach its potential customers. These periodic circulars are very professional, with clean-cut photographs of the merchandise. Beacon's mailings are unusually extensive, using its own customer lists as well as also purchasing additional lists from credit card organizations, etc. The company claims to have over eleven million mail-order customers and they do have a multi-million dollar annual sales volume.

In this instance, the mailing centered around four pairs of slacks and the photographs showed the fabrics and styling of the slacks very clearly. Two pairs of the slacks were in solid colors, suitable for the season; the other two pair were in small checks and came in several color combinations. The order blank that accompanied the circular requested the customer to specify waist size and in-seam lengths. The slacks, as usual, were pre-cuffed for length and the manufacturer, in accordance with the strict specifications on buying orders from Beacon's slacks' buyer, made them with in-seam lengths of 28", 29", 30", 31", and 32", because they were the most popular sizes to go with the waist sizes of 30–38".

The slacks were manufactured according to specifications and shipped to Beacon's. The response to the mailing was immediate and excellent. The Shipping Department worked overtime to rush the orders to customers, who visualized a bargain at $10 a pair.

However, within a matter of a week or so after the first orders were delivered to the customers, there was a rash of returns.

Incidentally, Beacon's had a well-known policy, plainly stated on the order blank: "Your money instantly refunded if you are not pleased." In fact, the flyer offered to give each customer one week's free trial—to wear the slacks and if not completely satisfied, to return the merchandise for refund without question.

Most customers included a letter with the returned slacks and almost unanimously the reason for the return was the same—the slacks' in-seam lengths were too short—they needed at least another half-inch and there was not enough fabric available to "let down" the cuffs. Beacon's sent a letter offering the next size in-seam length, but there were few takers because of the skimpiness of the fabric and the difficulty in alterations.

Ed Hawthorne, the slacks' buyer for Beacon's, rechecked his specifications and could not find anything in the instructions to provide for lengthening. But this did not prevent him from going to the manufacturer and remonstrating with him, hoping to find some way out of this situation.

Sam Schultz, one of the principals of the slacks manufacturing company, replied, "Look, Ed, these slacks were made to sell at a price. How can we sell a pair of slacks at $5.50 net made of 100% polyester double knit fabric with such great tailoring without some savings of fabric. We have to make a profit. Slacks can be made with a fabric allowance, but the price we agreed on was very low and you recognized that by not specifying the extra fabric as you almost always do. It allowed us to save money and bring in the slacks at a low price. If we did not save that money on the fabric, we couldn't sell them for the price you wanted. We went all over that when you negotiated the deal with me. Let's face it, if you had wanted a more liberal fabric allowance for the thousands of pairs of slacks, we would have charged more. Therefore, the responsibility is all yours."

What should Ed Hawthorne do?

Case 18
The Improvident
Cancellation

Fashion Rite Stores is a national women's apparel chain which features popular-priced merchandise. There are approximately two hundred stores which are located all over the country, but it is fair to say that they are concentrated primarily in the larger cities' downtown shopping areas and in suburban shopping centers. The home office of the chain as its central buying setup is located in New York City.

The fall season was approaching and Muriel Sharp, the dress buyer, was once again reviewing her fall plans. In particular, she was thinking about the order she had placed with Gay Apparel for twenty thousand dresses in three styles, for August 30 delivery, complete.*

Accordingly, on August 25, Mary Jane Sommerset, the assistant dress buyer of the Dress Department, in the course of following up on orders, visited the Gay Apparel showroom and in a friendly manner warned the sales manager that while they had an August 30, complete date, they were playing it too close for comfort in shipping the big order.

"You know," said Mary Jane, "that we don't really run a warehouse here in New York. All we do is check and ticket the dresses. We need time to do our paper distribution; pick the store orders; and pack and ship the goods to the stores. We were really hoping to have your dresses in around August 20 to give us a little more lead time for planning and distribution."

At the end of the day, Sommerset returned to the home office of Fashion Rite Stores and reported on her follow-up duties to her boss, Muriel Sharp. The buyer, who had spent the day in the office reviewing her figures with Neal Rodgers, her divisional merchandise manager, listened attentively.

It seems that Sharp realized that the entire chain's sales were

---

* Like all apparel chains, Fashion Rite Stores required complete delivery on their orders and refused to take partial shipments because of the need on the part of the chain's paper and physical distributors to be able to function properly. It also should be noted that the seemingly late delivery date of August 30, complete, was due to the fact that the chain's customers buy late—closer to need; department store delivery dates for fall are normally in late June to the end of July frequently into August, depending upon the nature of the operation and the location of the store. In addition, popular-priced chains such as Fashion Rite Stores buy primarily from "knock off" resources.

off; that retail business in general, throughout the country, was not good; and that the weather had been grim and not conducive to retail selling. There was the feeling that the market had not developed the right styling, a condition that requires later revision.

The Dress Department's stocks had backed up and stock sales ratios were way-out of proportion. This entire situation was certainly enough to worry both Rodgers and Sharp as well as the top management of the chain. They all came to the conclusion that the best thing to do was to cut back on outstanding orders whenever and wherever they could, so that they could come into the fall season as "light" as possible.

Everyone was in agreement that in view of the circumstances, the Dress Department's merchandise commitments (as well as the other departments) were out of line. In truth, therefore, they were looking for excuses to cancel orders.

After hearing Mary Jane's report, Sharp called Marvin Kowan, one of the principals of Gay Apparel.

At the end of the conversation, she said, "Marv, it looks as if you won't be able to make our August 30, complete, deadline. So let's get it over with and cancel the order now. We'll catch you on the next round—that's a promise."

"Over my dead body," fumed Kowan. "You know darn well that I have a large investment in fabric and labor on this order. Twenty thousand dresses is nothing to sneeze at. I'll break my back, but we'll be on time. . . ."

After hanging up, Sharp turned to Sommerset and said, "Send him a cancellation order, dated August 30, Mary Jane, and see to it that he gets it right on the nose."

Sure enough, Gay Apparel received the cancellation order exactly on August 30 when they had ninety-eight percent of the merchandise complete.

Kowan is sure that he can ship the full order by the next day. He calls Sharp, "Listen, Muriel, we've been doing business for a long time. I'm only missing a few pieces of one color. I expect to ship complete no later than tomorrow . . . only one day late. I don't have to remind you of the unwritten code in the trade—a manufacturer has up to three days extra time to ship. As a courtesy to me, I ask you to tear up this cancellation. Believe me, I know your situation; I know your business is off; but so is mine. Please don't hurt me this way on a little technicality."

Sharp replied, simply, "Marv, I don't want to argue with you. You're a day late—a day is a day—I'm sorry. I have to hold you to the order. That's the way it has to be. Sorry."

But Kowan persisted: "You're not being fair. I've been honest and aboveboard with you all these years and just because there's a temporary setback in business, you're sticking me with twenty thousand dresses. You just can't do this to me—I'm shipping the goods as ordered today."

Muriel Sharp came back quickly, "Listen, don't be stupid and throw good money after bad. If you ship those dresses, they won't be accepted by our receiving room and all you'll be doing is giving the dresses a round trip at your expense. And besides, play it smart. I promised to give you a big order on the next time around, remember? I must remind you also of future business as well."

Sure enough, on August 31, the goods were presented for delivery at the receiving platform of Fashion Rite Stores. But, without an order in the files, the shipment was refused. The order was taken to the holding room of the carrier after Gay Apparel also refused the merchandise claiming that title had passed to Fashion Rite.

Marvin Kowan was going to take a hard position.

Assume that you are a merchandise trainee of Fashion Rite Stores and have observed all the circumstances outlined. You are curious about:

1. The sanctity of the contract
2. The market relationship between buyers and selling in the chain market
3. The probable settlement terms of these issues
4. The manufacturer's alternatives

How do you think Muriel Sharp would respond to these subjects?

Case 19
Pity the Poor Manager

Metro Fashions, Inc. is a local women's apparel chain which has thirty stores within a twenty-five mile radius of the chain's central buying office and warehouse. The chain started doing business in small stores in the city's downtown financial district, in the railroad terminals, and in the vicinity of the larger office building complexes. Later, Metro expanded to nearby suburban shopping centers and other main streets in individual neighborhoods of the city. While some of the newer stores are larger, the average Metro store measures between twelve hundred and fifteen hundred square feet of selling space and carries typical promotional fashion merchandise.

The chain operates under the central merchandising plan with buyers and distributors controlling the purchasing and the flow of merchandise to each store. The store manager can only request certain items. Like other ready-to-wear chains, the buyers depend entirely on their records and, of course, this makes for a typical chain-home office-store impersonal relationship. There is also the typical selling apathy that is the result of absentee ownership, particularly when the store personnel is not enthusiastic about any item that is shipped to them.

Well aware of this situation, Paul Hill, president of Metro Fashions, has made it a policy for the chain's buyers, as an integral part of their job, to include frequent visits to the stores. While the home office is on a five-day week, the buyers are expected to visit the suburban stores on Saturday most of the year-round. And during the off-season buying periods when the buyers are not needed in the market they are expected to visit the center city stores.

During these visits, the buyers are required to work with the store managers as well as to give the salespeople merchandise information, and even occasionally assist in selling, so that they may be aware of customer reaction to the goods. Hill believes that such visits should go a long way to alleviating the impersonal feeling so prevalent in many chain stores.

Sid Warren, the store manager of Metro Fashions which was located in a nearby suburb, is well aware of these basic weaknesses and tries to do his best to cooperate with the home office. He knows his salespeople are not in the same league with the local, independent store owners, his principal competitors. In fact, despite Warren's many efforts, he realizes that the sales and stockkeeping aspects of his store are usually run by rudimentary people.

On this particular Saturday, Henrietta King, the handbag buyer, was in the store and was working with her senior handbag salesperson.

"Tillie," said King, "I don't pretend to memorize figures, but I could swear that your store was sent twenty-four pieces of these white straw bags from United Bag Company—style number 7283— and all I can see are three pieces on display."

"You mean this bag here with the big square gold clasp," Tillie replied. "Oh sure, we have them. There are at least fifteen or eighteen pieces in the stockroom."

"What do you mean—they're in the stockroom?" said the buyer in a horrified tone. "They belong here, up front, where people can see them. . . ."

"Oh no, no," replied Tillie. "I don't have room for them up front. I believe that our floor stock should be in proportion to what the customer is asking for. We have to make the best use of every available space. When a customer asks, we go into the stockroom and get a few more bags. These bags haven't moved too well, that's why I only have three up front."

"I bought these bags for Mother's Day," King replied. "You'll never sell many unless the customer is convinced that we have faith in this style, as evidenced by our willingness to invest in a number proportionate with our belief—that this is a winner."

The buyer runs to Sid Warren and gives him a piece of her mind concerning his salespeople's merchandising techniques. Warren replies that he cannot possibly look after each merchandise category and that he has to delegate such jobs to his individual department personnel.

The handbag buyer leaves in a huff, muttering threats over her shoulder to report the entire situation to Paul Hill, the president.

The manager shrugs his shoulders, mumbling, "Those buyers give me a pain. . . ."

Louise Haas, the lingerie buyer for Metro Fashions, is approaching the midtown store which is closest to the largest office building in the area. Haas checks the store's windows, which are the chain's chief means of sales promotion. She is looking for a special Mother's Day promotion, a group of brunch coats made from mattress ticking fabric that was featured in a leading women's periodical which has a huge circulation and which is sold only in supermarkets. To her chagrin, the brunch coat grouping was not on display, despite the fact that she, in cooperation with the chain's Display Department, had sent all the stores a bulletin together with a window banner and appropriate signs. The bulletin specifically showed how, when, and where to display this timely merchandise.

She stormed into the store seeking Elsie Robinson, the store manager, only to find that Robinson was out for coffee. Marjorie Laird, the assistant manager, was nearby and Haas gave her the full brunt of her anger.

"How do you expect to sell the thirty pieces I sent your store if nobody knows you have them?"

Trying to calm her down, Marjorie steered Haas to the Lingerie Department where the brunch coats were prominantly displayed up front.

While Haas calmed down a bit, she managed to say, "The windows get people into the store. They can't see or guess that we have these wanted items unless they're in the window. Paul Hill, our president, will get a full report from me. . . ."

On this same day, Lois Jasper, the hosiery buyer, was in the chain's newest and largest store which was located in a large, suburban shopping center. As she went over things in her department with the person in charge, she was reminded of an item that was on a point-of-sale display card and which was resting on a hosiery counter nearby. Jasper felt very fortunate in securing the novelty socks that the display card promoted. The big department stores had been advertising this merchandise and they had also been featured in a national teen-age magazine.

These novelty socks, knee high with unusually colored stripes just below the knee cuff, appealed to high school girls. They came in colors to coordinate or contrast with the short skirts or shorts being worn by this customer group.

When Jasper was able to secure a sufficient supply for each store, she sent a bulletin requesting store managers to give the socks display space: in the window, on the floor, on a leg form or on a mannequin with other coordinating merchandise.

Of course, this had not been done. There were no novelty socks on display and all that she saw was the manufacturer's counter display card.

When she asked the salesperson where the socks were, she was told that they were mixed in with the regular merchandise on the shelves behind the counter.

"If the customer asks for them, they're shown; sometimes we suggest them to a junior-miss type if she comes into the department."

When Jasper asked the store manager why he failed to follow the bulletin suggestions, he merely replied, "I have to use my own judgment. . . ."

In summary, not to "beat a dead horse" any further, with all the buyers making their store rounds, all jockeying for window space, front bargain tables, etc. and all filing lengthy reports with the president; and with the store managers, in turn, replying to these criticisms by writing reports or complaining to their district managers, the president soon realized that he must clarify things. Hill is quite aware of the situation in general. He calls a meeting with the other chain executives, including the buyers.

If you were Paul Hill, the president, what would you do?

VIII

THE RESIDENT BUYING OFFICE

DEFINITION

One of the most important communication links of fashion marketing is the resident buying office.

In a sense this institution is a staff department of the stores it represents since its basic function is to service its clientele or membership.

The term *buying* office is misleading because one could assume that an office is engaged to procure merchandise for retailers, and in a peripheral sense it has some validity. Factually, an RBO is a *service* organization that represents stores for three broad purposes:

1. Research
2. Buy with permission
3. Help to promote merchandise

Buying and achieving a profit is always the responsibility of the store buyer.

The definition of a resident buying office is a business organization that is located in a given fashion market and engaged to act as a market representative for a store, or group of stores, with its own complement of buyers. The word *representative* is the key to understanding the relationship.

HISTORICAL BACKGROUND

The resident buying office is a direct growth of socio-economic developments that followed World War I. In fact, these factors led to the birth of modern ready-to-wear and the necessity for the institution of resident buying:

1. The manufacturing of clothing reached mass production levels during the war because of the need for uniforms for both domestic and allied purposes. This new condition decreased the importance of home sewing and the neighborhood seamstress for children's and women's apparel.
2. The European social movement for female equality, which was imported to the U.S., and the entry of women into the mainstream of commercial life required styling suitable for business wear.
3. The technological developments of the cinema and the automobile resulted in new attitudes and needs for clothing.
4. The development of the urban population made for a fertile market, where masses of people could accept ideas, therefore clothing, of similar nature.
5. The other important ingredient was the product. Rayon was discovered a few years earlier and became available as a fabric for dresses at popular prices.

The picture was now complete—existing stores could now harvest the benefits. But, a new development in retailing took place —the apparel chain store—with advantages that challenged the entrenched department stores. The chains had:

1. Mass purchasing power
2. The ability to purchase in line with market developments since they operated from an office in the market itself

This competition worried the department stores that made sporadic market trips and had limited buying power. They needed relief to combat the apparel chain pressure.

As you might guess, the resident buying office was born— an institution that could represent the stores and make available group purchases to secure the advantages of mass purchasing power.

It is highly improbable that any store of even modest size can operate today without this service. Fashion merchandising is a unique business that requires timely merchandise in an ever changing market—what was good yesterday may be "old hat" today. Resident offices afford the opportunity to keep abreast of current developments and to stock merchandise in line with customer demand.

TYPES OF RESIDENT
BUYING OFFICES

The type of resident buying office a store uses, or can use, is a matter of the need, size, and nature of the operation. A large store with many departments doing high volume has different requirements from the specialty store doing a modest volume. To determine the guidelines for office selection, the reader is directed to: "Small Business Administration Marketers Aids," Pamphlet #116, Ernest Miller, who summarized many factors to be weighed in the selection of proper market representation.

The reader is also advised to refer to *Phelon's Resident Buying Book,* a book that lists all the resident offices in New York City, the personnel of the offices as well as member stores. You will observe that the salaried office (to be discussed) is the most numerous type, close to two hundred offices; in close second place, the merchandise broker office; the other types of resident offices are relatively fewer in number. There are five types of resident buying offices.

THE SALARIED OR INDEPENDENTLY OWNED OFFICE

The salaried or independently owned office receives remuneration from the represented stores, usually based on the volume of the store. Frequently, the fee is negotiated and a flat sum set.

THE MERCHANDISE BROKER (INDEPENDENTLY OWNED)

This office was at one time known as the *Commission Buying Office.* This type of office secures remuneration from the manufacturers on the basis of a percentage of the net shipment to a store. The store pays no fee. One of the considerations of a store is whether there is a conflict of office interest in order to obtain maximum revenue.

THE PRIVATE OFFICE (STORE OWNED)

This type of RBO is maintained by a store or group of stores to achieve a high level of efficiency and control their own personnel located in the marketplace. Private offices are, for the most part, located within an independent (salaried) or associated office.

THE ASSOCIATED OFFICE (COOPERATIVELY OWNED)

This office is jointly owned and managed by a group of stores having similarity of interest, size, ownership, needs; or any combination of these characteristics.

THE SYNDICATED OFFICE (CORPORATIVELY OWNED)

This type of resident buying office is owned by a corporation that owns the stores it services.

AVAILABLE OFFICE SERVICES

MARKET COVERAGE

Market representatives (sometimes referred to as "buyers") are the "eyes and ears" of the store buyer. They gather pertinent information which is relayed by bulletins, individual letters, in some cases telephone calls, and less frequently wires to all member stores.

Some RBO bulletin types (the titles will vary with the offices) are:

> *Merchandise News*
> *Special Attention*
> *Reorder*
> *Immediate Action*
> *Fashion Activity*

SEASONAL PREVIEW CLINICS

In a seasonal preview clinic, the buyer can review the merchandise selected by the representative to illustrate trends of the selling season. It can be held in the resident buying office if space is available, or at a nearby hotel.

During the meeting, recommendations are made regarding such subjects as: classification strengths, depth of purchases, stock peak dates, colors, resources.

BUYING SERVICES

As previously discussed, the store buyer has the responsibility for buying merchandise. However, there are instances when the buyer cannot be in the market to place an order advantageously.

There are several different kinds of orders that a store buyer can instruct the resident office representative to place.

1. *Special Order*—a commitment for a special customer that requires a personal visit to the manufacturer to insure required delivery.
2. *Reorders*—an additional order to replace merchandise that sold well. The RBO representative may be in a position to secure preferential or fast delivery, or place the order with another manufacturer making similar goods (with store buyer permission).
3. *Sample Order*—the placement of an order for new goods. The RBO representative must obtain permission from the store buyer before placing a commitment for newly developed styles in minimal quantities to include in stock to determine a rate of sale. The permission is based on the store buyer's respect for the representative's judgment.
4. *Open Order*—one that is given to the RBO representative with leeway. The store buyer's instructions may include one, or a combination, of these specifics: price of merchandise, specific colors, manufacturer, sizes, and delivery. What is detailed is dependent upon the store's need and the relationship between store buyer and representative.

COUNSELING SERVICES

Every office purports to render personalized service to its clients, that is to work on a one-to-one basis with buyers, merchandise managers, and top level management. At the buyer level, the personal relationship (both buyers working as a team) covers:

1. Discussions on particular store needs and market information tailored to the store.
2. Personal letters, as described.
3. Joint resource visits, particularly in the case of new buyers.
4. Store visits by the representative on occasions, particularly when the occasion demands objective evaluations.

UNIT CONTROL SERVICES

An extra service for an additional fee. The RBO acts as a chain operator for a department, buying without permission, maintaining records, and developing promotional means to sell the goods. The store is relieved of the merchandising responsibility and the department operates without a store buyer. The liaison in the store is a department manager. The department that operates under this method is usually one that features popularly priced merchandise.

GROUP BUYING PROGRAMS AND WHOLESALE ACTIVITIES

Pooling orders and buying in large quantities has one or as many as three advantages:

1. Special price (including co-op advertising)
2. Exclusivity (often specification merchandise)
3. Delivery (preference to large users)

The larger offices usually have *steering committee meetings* that are attended by selected buyers of member stores who represent all the member stores. They decide to either develop new merchandise or pool orders for recommended items to obtain some advantages.

Another group activity is operated by office personnel—*wholesaling*—for the purpose of gaining an advantage for their store members. A program could be directed to obtain special prices, scarce goods (most often classic products), preferred delivery, etc. Some offices maintain a separate corporate entity that operates as a jobber, charging participating stores (that use the goods) a small percentage for the service. Under these programs two classes of goods may be developed: private brands and foreign merchandise.

SALES PROMOTION SERVICES

This merchandising service is an important phase that helps the stores to "move" goods, the activity that must take place to secure a profit.

The following are commonly offered to clients:

1. *Ad Mats*—provide clients with tailored artwork and text to advertise in newspapers.
2. *Statement Enclosures (with store logo imprinted)*—suitable for mailing to customers, often at less than cost prices because they could be subsidized by manufacturers.
3. *Displays*—obtained from magazines or display authorities with themes often developed by the office fashion coordinator.
4. *Catalogues*—office developed with manufacturer finan-

cial support, and available with store logo imprinted at costs well below commercial rates obtainable by individual stores.

5. *Fashion Office Services*—the fashion coordinator constantly develops ideas for fashion shows, fashion kits, window displays (as indicated), and on occasion, visits stores (by store request) to stage a show. Where radio and television time is available, the coordinator can appear as a guest and secure added fashion flavor for the store.

MISCELLANEOUS SERVICES

1. Effecting exchanges, cancellations and adjustments of orders and merchandise.
2. Making sample rooms in the resident office available during market trips to save the buyer's time.
3. Visiting the store to handle store problems, as stated. Some trip can include representatives, merchandise managers, and top level management of the office.
4. Effecting exchange of merchandising information among member stores.
5. Recruiting personnel for the store, from trainees to managers.
6. Supplying personal services requested by store personnel such as hotel accommodations, tickets for entertainment. Of course, these services are paid for by the store or the personnel requesting same, depending upon the request.

ORGANIZATION OF A RESIDENT BUYING OFFICE

An organization chart for a resident buying office is dependent upon the clientele it serves. In a larger office servicing giant stores, there must be many levels of responsibility and a wide range of buyers and staff because there must be office coverage for all store personnel. It is easiest to say, that every member of a store has a counterpart in the RBO and that they consult during market trips, and in the case of higher store levels, when annual meetings are held.

The line of organization, therefore, of a typical ready-to-wear office operation is:

- General Merchandise Manager
- Divisional Merchandise Manager

- Buyer
- Assistant Buyer
- Follow-up Assistant

In conclusion, the resident buying office is a necessary adjunct of a store, particularly in fashion merchandising where the roots of its establishment were first planted.

An RBO should not be confused with a chain operation which merchandises its own stores; in which operation, the stores in reality service the home office. At all times, the resident buying office must be considered a complete service organization and the buyers are representatives who act for the store buyers as a service arm.

Case 20
Should All the Eggs
Go in One Basket?

Lawrence Collins is the president of a chain store operation consisting of nine popular-priced units located in West Virginia. The main office is in Charleston and operates with four buyers who visit the New York market approximately six times a year. The exception is Rose Treadwell who handles dresses and sportswear; she is in New York every two months. The total volume of the Dress and Sportswear Departments is $600,000 a year, of which dresses contributes $250,000.

Even though Treadwell's formal training is limited, having come up from the ranks as a salesperson, she is considered a dedicated, fairly knowledgeable merchandiser.

Collins, although satisfied with her performance, believes that the chain is not obtaining its full share of volume potential. He has never entertained the thought of replacing Treadwell, because he is essentially a small-town man who believes in loyalty and appreciates that trait in his buyers. In fact, Treadwell is unmarried and considers her job the largest part of her life.

Collins was in New York last week and reviewed his operation with the management staff of his resident buying office, Associated Small Stores, Inc. In addition to Collins, Leonard Carroll, the president, and Marvin Black, the merchandise manager of popular-priced apparel, were present.

During the meeting, Carroll, a dynamic businessman, suggested that the Collins chain join the office's unit control service.

His remarks included: "The central operation is a store economy, a buyer is not needed, and the fee is only 2% of net sales. You can make your buyer a department manager. We can give you a sharp operation by controlling the merchandise plans, buying, furnishing ad mats and above all, stocking merchandise in popular demand."

Carroll's arguments were so powerful and logical that Collins' sense of loyalty began to waver and he was on the verge of saying, "Give me the contract and I'll sign up for a year." But, his business acumen dictated a cautious approach. He decided to mull it over before coming to a conclusion.

He then sought out his trusted long-time office controller, John

Slattery, a vice president and a level-headed pragmatist.

After listening to what had transpired, Slattery said, "The economics of the situation are probably as presented by Associated; we might be better off using the service. However, you realize that there are two negative points. One, you're going to 'destroy' Rose Treadwell who will never accept the job of department manager; and two, what does a New York controller who will dictate what we can sell know about the local conditions in West Virginia."

Collins replied, "John, you're saying just what I've been thinking and I'm up a tree. I'll have to give this matter some more consideration."

If these facts were presented to you, how would you handle the matter?

Case 21
Ethics

Fashion Limited is one of the numerous New York resident buying offices servicing small stores. Its clientele is concentrated in New Jersey, Pennsylvania, and Maryland.

One of the member stores is Vogue of Baltimore, owned by Sam Schwartz, a former buyer of Woodward and Lothrop of Washington, D.C. After fifteen years of larger store merchandising, he opened Vogue and has had a good measure of success. Schwartz knows how to work with the resident buyers who he visits every three to four weeks. He has discussions with them, states his problems with accuracy, and spends little time on small talk. He has no time for any social graces, market or office gossip.

About two weeks ago, he received an office "reorder" bulletin that included two dress styles from Adam's Fashions, a resource held in low esteem by Schwartz. He had used them on several occasions and had come to the conclusion that they are secondary makers. Their fit was less than satisfactory, the delivery performance poor, and the retail selling mediocre.

He could not comprehend why a market specialist would recommend Adam's. A call to a friendly competitor justified his feelings. In an attempt to be fair and, because he had no recent merchandise from Adam's, he visited the company and reviewed the line, including the "reorder" styles.

"I'll be darned," he said. "If these are reorder styles, I'll eat them. The buyer, Florence Robinson, must be in on the 'take'; she's too smart to tout these 'dogs.'"

Although stubborn and opinionated, Schwartz is far from stupid. He knows that if he tells the resident buying office president he may lose the war, since there will be a breach in relationship with the buyer. The other possibility is that Florence Robinson would be fired. He also knows that he is never going to prove that the buyer is taking money; she will not confess and the manufacturer will not talk.

If you were Sam Schwartz, what would you do? Remember, he is paying for honest, professional service, and depending upon it for decisions that could be unfair and dangerous to the operation.

Case 22
The Catalogue

Merchandise Planners Associates, Inc. is a salaried resident buying office with a membership roll of two hundred and twenty accounts, most of which are second- or third-rated stores in their respective locales. Merchandise Planners is a live wire resident buying office and a money-making company. One of their important sources of revenue is the Promotion Department. It prepares ad mats, bulletins, and catalogues for the member stores. Mats and bulletins, supported by manufacturers, are sent to the stores free. The catalogue costs are borne by manufacturers and stores. The latter receives them with the stores' logos imprinted at minimum costs, well below individual preparation costs. Catalogues are offered at least three times a year: spring, fall, and holiday.

The Del Mar Store of Gary, Indiana, is a new account in the office, having signed a contract three months ago. Actually, their contract with another buying office is still in effect with the result that Del Mar is paying two fees. The reason for this situation is that Merchandise Planners was open for an account in Gary and was conducting negotiations with Del Mar and a competitor. The management of Del Mar was anxious for Merchandise Planners service and signed first, thus eliminating the competitor.

The store buyers, because of temporary dual representation, are just becoming acquainted with the new resident representative. It might be said that the Del Mar buyers are biased in favor of the services of the former office. Their feeling is that Merchandise Planners concentrates too heavily on popular- to medium-priced goods.

One month ago, Merchandise Planners sent out a powerful bulletin describing the merchandise, resources, deliveries, and other necessary details of the Christmas catalogue. It is priced very low, $5.00 per thousand, and looks as if it will be a quality catalogue. Since Del Mar distributes fifty thousand catalogues, which accelerates business considerably, the merchandise investment is of major proportions.

John Scully, the ready-to-wear merchandise manager, after studying the bulletin called Sylvia Lash, the sportswear buyer and senior member of the merchandise staff.

"What do you think of it," he asked.

"Not for us," she said. "It's too cheap."

"This is a typical department store catalogue. Our customers want better goods, particularly during the holiday period."

Scully was somewhat perplexed. The merchandise was at the medium to slightly above levels, appeared to be from well-known makers that had been stocked frequently by the store. His reaction was that there must be an ulterior motive.

He therefore responded, "Aren't you being unfair."

"Not at all, facts are facts," was Sylvia's reply.

"Well," he said, "it looks as if you'll have to live with our choice, we want this catalogue."

With hands on hips and pursed lips, she stated, "Then you'll have to buy the goods, I won't."

It must be noted that Lash has a fine store record of long standing and knows she will not be fired. She is good, knows it, and is highly employable.

Scully is not without strength either. He is a valuable employee, owns stock in the company, and is a member of the store's management board.

You are John Scully. Analyze the situation and select the alternative you feel responds best to the situation.

FASHION BUYING FOR THE SMALL INDEPENDENT STORE

DEFINITION

A small store is one that is difficult to define. The definition depends upon the basis of comparison.

Estimations indicate that there are about 1,500,000 small stores, approximately 88% of all retail units.

For our purpose, we will use the standard of ownership. Therefore, our discussion will center on the independent establishment that is a one-store operation, usually a one-person firm, or partnership, in which all the functions of retailing are performed by the owner (or owners).

This book concentrates on the merchandising phase of retailing; and that is the nub of the discussion of this chapter. When one establishes a store, the responsibilities include merchandising plus all the functions of retailing such as financing, credit extension, receiving, marking of goods, keeping records, and all other necessary operations.

Failure rate among small store owners is extremely high due to lack of experience. This deficiency is not confined to newcomers to the field of fashion merchandising; it also pertains to seasoned large store merchandisers whose experiences are confined to the activities described in this book—planning, buying and selling. There are substantive differences between merchandising in a large organization and operating a small business.

Here are some of the characteristics inherent in a small operation; some advantages and disadvantages:

BUYING AND MERCHANDISING

Smallness does not lend closeness or importance to leading fashion manufacturers; and in some cases, the store owner cannot purchase merchandise from desired resources. It is the larger organization that influences a trading area and receives preferential delivery and, sometimes, exclusivity of best styles.

The small store owner enjoys the advantage of more precise knowledge of his customers. His buying can be streamlined to suit the needs of his patrons. On the other hand, pinpointing new styles for a selective audience takes considerable expertise.

A major disadvantage is the inability to sell off buying mistakes. Limited traffic makes it difficult to recognize mistakes and to markdown and eliminate them.

FINANCE AND CONTROL

The store owner is rarely an expert in the proper handling of accounts, financing, and risk taking. Additionally, limited capital affords limited bank credit. If the ownership is incorporated, a bank may refuse credit facilities unless the owner assumes personal liability, even for modest sums. Undercapitalization is one of the pitfalls for all small businesses; one bad season can spell failure.

OPERATIONS AND MANAGEMENT

Smallness is synonymous with generalization. A well-structured large operation has specialists in every area; the small store is run by someone who fulfills the tasks. As an example, large stores have a traffic manager who obtains the cheapest and most efficient means of transportation of merchandise; the small operator, who has little knowledge and limited size shipments, may become the victim of the people with whom he does business.

In the area of management, a perceptive owner can be highly efficient and often offers personal service and customer satisfaction, no small advantage.

PROMOTIONAL ACTIVITY

The disadvantage is clear; high costs of newspapers, catalogues and radio can make them prohibitive means of promotions. Even if costs can be absorbed, artists, copy experts, and layout artists are not part of the staff.

Most individual store owners use the mail and telephone to best advantage, another personal touch. A small operator with a fashion flair can run fashion shows for local charities, or mailings to stimulate demand and customer patronage. These events influence consumers and they believe that a store is being operated by a fashion expert.

The larger operations use promotional means for special events to clear end-of-season stocks and accelerate selling for most events.

LOCATION

A good location is usually one that offers high customer traffic. One hundred percent locations are expensive and usually beyond the means of the small business person. Since World War II, this situation has become more complex because of the shifting nature of the population; which has caused even new suburban areas to deteriorate.

Limited capital can prevent mobility. Therefore the location within the means of the individual entrepreneur is often less than desired and necessitates strategies not offered by competition to attract patrons. The constant practice of creativity is exciting but it may require more perseverance than the practitioner anticipates or is able to perform.

PHYSICAL ASPECTS

When one is part of an organization, there is assignment and responsibility for a limited number of duties. In a small store, there is an implied marriage between the owner and the business; it is a relationship that demands full-time presence and strict attention. This must be a realization of a new owner, because anything less can be the difference between success and failure.

Here is a list of selected considerations that face the small retailer:

1. Should brands be carried.
2. How to balance stocks that are limited.
3. How is inventory controlled with limited buying power.
4. Should customer credit be extended with limited capital and high cost of bank rates.
5. How much insurance should be carried.
6. How to prevent shoplifting in a small store.

7. How to promote goods with a small budget.
8. Does one hire sales help when sales are limited.
9. How does one build a fashion reputation.
10. What is the small retailer's means of presenting special events.
11. What is the approach to the customer return of goods (refund or credit).
12. How does one meet competition.

The entrepreneur in America is not dead. There are many opportunities for the ambitious who are willing to pay the price of total involvement. An advantage is the realization of the American dream—to own one's own business. The opportunity to be creative and receive the returns for efforts are the rewards.

Case 23
The Small Store
Dilemma

You are a small store owner in Des Moines, Iowa. The yearly volume is in the neighborhood of $300,000 which yields a comfortable living. Your sales personnel consists of one full-time salesperson and one part-timer, a student at the local community college. The customers are in the middle to slightly above average income range. They are not fashion leaders in the sense that they want the latest market offerings, but they are fashion conscious and highly selective.

You enjoy running the store. It adds up to a most pleasant and profitable occupation. That is until six months ago when you learned that one of the major stores in the state, with a national reputation, had filed plans to build a shopping center approximately a quarter of a mile from your location. It will be ready for occupancy in eight months. The main store of the shopping center will be a larger branch unit. This has upset you; you know that the ladies' sportswear and dress departments will be in direct competition to the merchandise classifications you carry.

Even though you know the character and practices of the department store, you start an in-depth investigation. You find that the store and the departments offer a wide assortment of styles, maintain depth beyond your ability, have interesting and compelling ads of the right styles, offer personal selling service, and maintain liberal return policies.

You are in a quandary. You know that there is a possibility that you will not be able to stand the pressure.

One of your neighbors, the owner of a children's shop, remarked the other day, "I know what I'm going to do—look for another location. I can't stand up to the competition."

Your full-time salesperson, Sara Cummings, keeps repeating, "I'm not afraid of them. They're big, but our customers are loyal. They've been our customers for several years and they like us."

However, you are not convinced. Your location is in a strip shopping area with no strong pull from adjoining stores. Your strength has to come from within. You must take steps to ensure your continued success. As a small store operator, you know that you cannot obtain exclusivity of styling, preferential delivery, buy in promotional quantity or use conventional promotional power.

You visit your resident buying office, an operation that handles small specialty shops, but you feel that their advice is inadequate to meet the situation. As a matter of fact, you are somewhat annoyed by the president's suggestion, "Visit the market more often." Unrealistic was your reaction. You think, as a small store operator, how can I visit New York frequently. It is too costly, I do not have the volume to support frequent purchases, and how will it put me in a better position?

If you were the small store operator, what course of action would you take?

Case 24
An Overstocked
Condition

La Modeste is a ladies', men's and children's specialty shop in suburban Mansfield, Ohio, a middle- to upper-income level area. The owner, Dale Phelon, inherited the business from his father who founded it thirty years ago. The store is the dominant fashion operation in the town and attracts customers as far away as fifteen to twenty miles. It features the latest styles at moderate to better prices, charge accounts, free deliveries, gift wrappings and naturally, full personal services. It is an example of a smart successful operation that has reached a volume of $3.5 million.

Two months ago, the better dress buyer took ill and was hospitalized, after which she was confined to her home. The store has no assistant buyers therefore the department has been functioning without a department head.

A week ago, the owner was examining the records and noted that the better dress figures were off 30%. Phelon visited the department and spoke to the two salespeople. They calmly informed him that the reason for the drop-off was the selection of dresses, predominately black. They realized that it is late October and the need for dark styles, but why stock merchandise that looks like mourning dresses.

"How did this happen," Phelon asked.

"Well," replied one of the salespeople, "your wife has been filling in stock, and she buys mostly black with a few navies."

Phelon was nonplussed. He thought of his wife, a part-time employee, as a shrewd merchant who should know better. He realized she was filling in, really did not give the task her fullest attention, and that it has been considerable time since she had a grasp of dress merchandising.

Two days ago, he contacted you, a senior dress buyer at the nearest department store, a noncompetitive retailer.

During the phone conversation he said, "You're an old friend and I would consider it a favor if you visited my store this Sunday for an hour or so and looked the situation over."

On Sunday at 9 A.M., you arrived at the store, which was opened just for the occasion. You reviewed the stock, and indeed, it looked terrible. It was loaded with black and a few navies. The situation looked bad.

"How bad?" Phelon asked.

"Pretty bad."

"What do I do now, and how much is it going to cost? Remember I'm still a specialty shop. I can advertise but they won't come in droves. More than that, if I go all-out in an ad, or ads, they'll buy nothing but promotional goods in a peak volume period. What do I do to get right?"

As a seasoned merchandiser you know that he is right. A specialty shop, even though it is fairly large, cannot bring traffic into the store to move major mistakes in a hurry. In addition, a fashion store running strong ads at markdown prices in a peak selling period could encounter trouble. The dilemma is how to get rid of hundreds of dresses without looking as if the store experts did not know how to buy fashions, regain selling momentum of the right goods, and not take too big a loss.

You weigh the situation very carefully because you have a genuine desire to help Phelon, a fine man for whom you have a great deal of respect.

Analyze the situation, giving pros and cons, and select an alternative which in your opinion is the course of action that should be followed.

Case 25
The Entrepreneurs

Mike Freedman and Mary Birmingham were college class-mates who were graduated last June. They are both interested in fashion merchandising and cannot visualize themselves as employees of a large organization. They decided that opening their own store is their "bag."

After graduation they spoke to their parents who, though not delighted at the prospect of lending them money, agreed to each advance $15,000 on a long-term basis, ten years, at an interest rate of five percent, to start one year after the store's opening.

Mike and Mary were overjoyed. They immediately started to look for a location in the suburban areas of Long Island and West-chester County. After a week, a friend tipped them off to a store that was up for "grabs." It seems that the owner, sixty-two years old, is in questionable health and wants to retire. The store, they were told, has always been a money-maker as evidenced by the owners mode of living and his total dependency on the store for income.

The young couple made contact and looked the store over. The store is in the heart of Fairfield, Connecticut's main shopping area, with a thirty foot front and sixty foot depth.

The volume, although not in a present growth situation, shows an average of $150,000 per annum. The rent is $12,000 a year based on a lease that extends for another five years and a renewal clause for its extension for another five years at a yearly increase of 5%.

The asking price is $75,000, which Mike's father, a business-man, judged as being a good buy. The owner is willing to take back a purchase money mortgage on easy terms, spread over ten years.

The terms, cost of store, rent, location, size, are compatible with the means and desires of the couple, with one exception. Mary pointed out that the success of the store was really based on the merchandising of men's suits, which was helped by men's furnish-ings.

She said, "We don't want to be in the men's area, although we probably could do well in sportswear, but not suits. We know nothing about that area and we could get killed."

Mike, after reflection said, "You could be right, so why not just eliminate suits. We're forced to buy the stock, but we could clear it out and use the money to stock ladies' apparel and some additional new furnishings."

"One problem," retorted Mary. "Do you realize that there are several shops in the area carrying female apparel. The store may not have been successful if there had been competition."

Mike said, "Now, you have me worried."

You were a classmate, and Mike and Mary have made you privy to their negotiations.

Analyze the situation for them since they have lost their objectivity.

ASSISTING THE BUYER OR STEPS LEADING TO THE POSITION OF BUYER

This chapter is devoted to those who assist the buyer in buying, merchandising as well as management functions. We have already discussed those who have similar positions in the chain and resident buying office. And, again, because they make up the preponderance of such positions in the fashion buying and merchandising fields, we return to the large specialty or department store for this study. Here, too, will be found the greatest variety of responsibilities. It should be noted that the following descriptions are all inclusive and not necessarily those of every assistant; as indicated, the size, organizational structure, and nature of the operation will make for variations of duties.

THE ASSISTANT BUYER

The assistant buyer as the title implies, assists the buyer in many of his buying and merchandising duties. (The reader is cautioned about this title—there is a similar-sounding one—*assistant-to-the-buyer*—which is a clerical position.) The assistant buyer is generally a college-educated person who has been selected and who is being trained for an executive position, such as buyer.

The assistant buyer has many major responsibilities including:

1. *Buying*
   A. Advise the buyer on current sales and style trends; also on the purchase of merchandise.
   B. Handle reorders and special orders.
   C. Accompany the buyer to local markets; occasionally to major markets; perhaps visit the market alone to survey and report trends.
   D. Handle purchase order cancellations and returns-to-vendor (R.T.V.).

2. *Merchandising*
   A. Handle markup and markdown procedures.
   B. Handle stock control, stock records, and unit control.
   C. Supervise physical inventory and periodic stock counts.
   D. Study and analyze daily, monthly and seasonal reports to determine and inform the buyer of slow- and fast-moving items.

3. *Systems and Procedures*
   A. Supervise (spot check) salespeople's handling of cash register, sales checks, etc.
   B. Supervise the Selling Cost Percent figures—helps to set and supervise the attainment of daily and weekly sales quotas.

4. *Receiving and Marking*
   A. Establish a regular routine on a daily basis in checking on incoming merchandise.
   B. Maintain daily contact with receiving room personnel to insure quickest process of receiving and delivery to departments.
   C. Allocate marked merchandise to stock areas or selling floor.

5. *Stockkeeping*
   A. Delegate daily stock duties to subordinates.
   B. Supervise stock arrangements on selling floor.

6. *Sales Activities*
   A. Give the buyer interpretation of customer wants and opinions.
   B. Train or re-train salespeople—individually or at meetings—on selling techniques.
   C. Motivate salespeople.
   D. Supervise want slips system.

7. *Personnel*
   A. Maintain adequate floor coverage in line with budgetary conditions.

  B. Take a hand in the evaluation of the department's personnel.
  C. Help to make the new employee feel at home.
  D. Take part in the training of new employees; retraining of old employees.
 8. *Sales Promotion*
  A. Change department displays.
  B. Supervise department signs.
  C. Help to select merchandise for window display.
  D. Circulate among salespeople copies of merchandise advertised in the newspaper prior to the sale date.
 9. *Operations*
  A. Supervise the requisition and use of supplies for the department.
  B. Observe and teach salespeople safety precautions.
  C. Keep the salespeople up-to-date on credit procedures; delivery, wrapping, and packing problems; review the handling of exchanges, refunds, and other adjustments.
 10. *The Future*
  A. Learn the duties of the buyer or the associate buyer in order to be able to take over either position on a temporary or a permanent basis.
  B. Prepare to assume more responsibility from the day the job as assistant buyer is begun.
  C. The assistant buyer's job is the cornerstone of a career in buying.

THE ASSOCIATE BUYER

The associate buyer, sometimes called the senior assistant buyer, is the understudy for the buyer. She is also the buyer's right hand in all phases of the buying function, frequently being assigned to buy a distinct segment of the department's merchandise. The associate buyer is also thought of as the next buyer of the department or any other department she is qualified to head. The associate buyer, unlike the assistant buyer when she first begins, must be knowledgeable about all the factors that go into running a fashion merchandise department.
 1. *Merchandising*
  A. Know all the merchandise of the department and the records that control that merchandise.
  B. Know how to merchandise stock for better turnover.

      C. Understand dollar and unit planning.

      D. Maintain, study, and use all department records.

2. *Buying*

      A. Write orders, special orders, on basic as well as new merchandise, under the buyer's supervision, where necessary.

      B. Know the department's resources.

      C. Follow up on orders, cancel where necessary.

      D. Be able to step into the buyer's job at a moment's notice for any reason.

3. *Sales Promotion*

      A. Give the Advertising Department copy information and samples of the merchandise to be sketched or photographed.

      B. Maintain sales records of merchandise that has been advertised.

      C. Supervise department signs.

      D. Keep salespeople informed on all advertised merchandise.

4. *Supervision*

      A. Generally make presence felt on sales floor as one of the nominal sales supervisors.

      B. In general, direct the work and the responsibility of the assistant buyer and the branch assistant buyer.

BRANCH STORE ASSISTANT BUYER

    It is a well-established fact that the population growth of the past several decades was accompanied by a mass movement of the population to the suburbs of most major American cities, resulting in a tremendous proliferation of branch stores. As the branches grew in number and size, the main store buyer's need for assistance became apparent. A new position was created which is sometimes called branch store coordinator, branch store merchandise controller or branch store assistant buyer. Your authors prefer the last title because it comes closest to typifying the position. It should be clearly understood that the branch assistant buyer *works* with the buyer *at the main store* and acts as the buyer's representative for all matters concerning branch store merchandising, services and supplies. The branch assistant buyer, in this liaison position, is also expected to provide both the buyer and the branch store department manager with merchandise information garnered from all parties concerned.

To be of effective use to the buyer, the branch assistant buyer must be knowledgeable in some of the following areas:

1. Understand and use merchandise control records.
2. Know how to recognize under- or overstock conditions as well as how to rectify them.
3. Transfer stock when and where necessary
4. Plan, expedite, and coordinate branch store sales and stock.
5. Establish good relationships with department managers in all branches.

In addition to the general areas of knowledge mentioned previously, the branch assistant buyer has a number of specific responsibilities:

1. Maintain records on branch store sales and stocks including good and poor selling items.
2. Provide branches with advertised merchandise.
3. Transfer slow-selling merchandise; keep records on all such transfers.
4. Select merchandise for shipment to branches based upon department records and sales plan; keep staple stock filled at all times.
5. Keep branch department managers informed on interesting or new merchandise; act as an information center for the branch stores.
6. Visit branch stores as often as possible both to observe and to create personal contacts with the branch store people.

BRANCH STORE DEPARTMENT MANAGER

The branch store department manager is another member of the department's merchandising/management team. This is being written on the relatively safe assumption that practically every large store has one or more branches. In fact, some of the country's biggest and best-run stores generally promote the main store assistant buyer to this position as part of their advancement schedule.

Some of the responsibilities of the branch store department manager include:

1. *Merchandising*
   A. Make certain that the right merchandise best suited for the branch's customers continues to arrive from the main store.

    B. Reorder basic stocks as well as current styles where available.

    C. Transfer slow-selling merchandise.

    D. Recommend items for promotion, numbers to markdown, and depth of stock.

    E. Send a continuing flow of information to the main store concerning shortages of stock, when to peak stock, stock counts, etc.

2. *Personnel*

    A. Work with the branch store management in such personnel areas as:

      (1) Ratings

      (2) Sponsor systems

      (3) Hiring, transfers, dismissal, promotions, etc.

    B. Train the department's personnel.

3. *Selling*

    A. Keep salespeople informed not only on the selling features of advertised and displayed items but on all other merchandise as well.

    B. Train and supervise salespeople in basic selling techniques from meeting the customer to closing the sale.

4. *Sales Promotion*

    A. Display

      (1) Order, secure, and be responsible for the accuracy of all signs.

      (2) Select items for display.

    B. Advertising

      (1) Be sure that there is sufficient merchandise to back up the advertisements.

      (2) Be certain that all department personnel know what is being advertised.

      (3) Recommend items for future advertisements.

      (4) Keep records of sales results of each advertisement.

5. *Miscellaneous*

    A. Work with Comparison Shopping Office.

    B. Work with operations division on maintenance and repairs; receiving and marking; and alterations and other work rooms.

    C. Take charge of housekeeping and stockkeeping functions of the department.

    D. Supervise handling of customer complaints, adjustments, refunds, and exchanges.

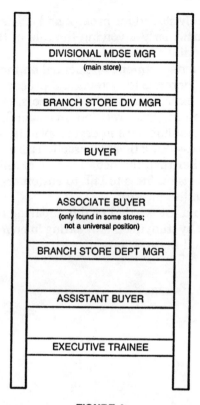

DIVISIONAL MDSE MGR
(main store)

BRANCH STORE DIV MGR

BUYER

ASSOCIATE BUYER
(only found in some stores;
not a universal position)

BRANCH STORE DEPT MGR

ASSISTANT BUYER

EXECUTIVE TRAINEE

FIGURE 4

THE SERVICE MANAGER*

It is agreed, at the outset, that the service manager is *not* a buying and merchandising executive. In fact, the service manager reports to the store manager who heads the Operations Division. However, your authors feel that this analysis of the staff that assist the buyer would be incomplete without a brief study of the service manager's position because his primary responsibility involves the supervision of the selling function as well as the salespeople engaged therein. And no one can deny that selling is an integral part of merchandising.

"If everything that is bought must be sold," then the following responsibilities of the service manager are noteworthy:

1. Determine personnel coverage needed and in accordance with budgetary allowances, insure that the department is

---

* In some stores, the Service Manager may also be called the Section Manager or Divisional Superintendent.

adequately staffed for prompt and efficient customer service, particularly involving the sale of the department's merchandise.

2. Keep the department's personnel on their toes by supervising adherence to systems and procedures, correct selling techniques, the work of sponsors, etc.

3. Act as the customer relations manager for the buyer insofar as handling customer complaints, adjustments, returns, etc.—using these transactions to emphasize the positive rather than the negative side of selling. In addition, make it his business to talk to customers on any phase of merchandise interest.

4. Develop a knowledge of the department's merchandise not only by studying but by sitting in on meetings with the buyer and his assistants.

Case 26
Branch Store Problem

Evelyn Gold is the sport coat buyer at Fletcher's Department Store, which is located in a large West Coast metropolitan area. As fashion dictated at the moment, her department handled such classifications as car coats, pea jackets, loden coats, storm coats, leisure coats, suburban coats. Most of the coats sold in this department retailed between $49 and $79.

Gold had been with Fletcher's for more than forty years, starting in the stockroom at eighteen. She was now approaching sixty, but in a futile gesture, she never admitted to being more than forty-three years old. Actually, Evelyn Gold was an anachronism that time had left behind. She was primarily main-downtown-store oriented, despite the fact that Fletcher's ten branches combined did more in sales volume than the old downtown store. As a result, the Sport Coat Departments in the branch stores were quite shamefully neglected and poorly stocked with the wrong merchandise because Gold was insensitive to their individual needs.

This was especially true insofar as the relatively new Purdy Springs store was concerned. This branch was located in an affluent, entirely middle class suburban area and it had already exceeded the projected sales volume. Management had revised their figures upward several times during the first year of business. Only the Sport Coat Department was doing poorly and there was some fretting about this. Gold had never visited the Purdy Springs store since she did not drive and the store was inaccessible by public transportation. Purdy Springs could easily sell sport coats in the $150 to $175 class but, of course, Gold never responded to the branch store department manager's pleas for better merchandise for her customers.

Pat Morris was the Purdy Springs branch store department manager with the Sport Coat Department under her supervision. Pat was a young, married woman, college graduate, who had been a member of Fletcher's executive training squad. She had been an assistant buyer in sportswear before being promoted to the department manager's position at the new Purdy Springs branch.

She, like all the other junior executives she had to deal with, was deeply resented by Gold for her attractive appearance, good education, rapid promotion, and swinging life style. Gold reminded herself constantly when she saw these younger managers that she had worked for Fletcher's as a stock- and salesperson in the old days before she had come within reach of her present position as buyer.

And Gold was well aware that she was one of the last of a dying breed.

Fletcher's top management knew that there were several buyers such as Evelyn Gold who were still around but they hesitated to terminate their tenure because of the decades of loyalty and devotion they had invested in the store and their jobs. There was also a question of morale that would probably seep down to the rank-and-file should the buyers be dismissed; and it would seem unwise to do such a thing in view of the fact that the bulwark of the store's personnel was composed of long-term employees, too.

Pat Morris, after a number of attempts to persuade Evelyn Gold to bring in better merchandise for Purdy Springs, such as expensive imports or fur-trims, had about given up. She despaired because her affluent customers were literally turning their noses up at the plebian offerings of the Sport Coat Department.

In a last-ditch attempt, Pat tried to get Evelyn to the local market where perhaps the excitement of the moment might make Gold feel that the needed merchandise was her own idea. But, of course, Evelyn did not fall for this scheme either. She had made it a point never to take any of her assistants into the market to begin with. In fact, Gold had a fundamental policy of keeping her subordinates in the dark as much as possible. In her insecurity, she felt that if these young managers knew too much, they would pose even a greater threat to her job.

Finally, Pat Morris realized that she could not get anywhere with her hard-nosed superior and that she would never make any headway in securing adequate merchandise for her store. She began to collect ads from both local independent stores and the branch stores of Fletcher's larger competitors. These ads clearly indicated the upgraded sport coat selections being offered in higher price ranges.

On one of her regularly scheduled weekly visits to the main store (a visit ordained by top management and one that Gold could not prevent, although she would have liked to), Morris presented her case to Jack Klein, the divisional merchandise manager, thereby going over Gold's head. Klein, who is aware of what has been going on only from what he can learn by studying the department's records, promised Pat that he would give the matter careful attention.

Unfortunately, Klein is not too tactful and Gold learned that he has been primed for his investigation by Pat Morris' assistance and at her instigation. Of course, Gold is furious and she soon let Pat Morris know that Fletcher's is not big enough for both of them.

If you were in Pat Morris' position, what would you do?

Case 27
Big Fish in
a Little Pond. . . .

Murray Green and Herbert Brown both started on the executive training squad at Wilson's Department Store in New York City on the same day.

Murray had earned his baccalaureate degree at a local school; and he had "worked his way through college" by being employed part-time at Wilson's, first as a stockperson and then as a salesperson in the Boys' Department. The enthusiastic recommendation of Ronald Black, the merchandise manager of the men's and boys' wear division, had helped him gain a place on the store's executive training squad, which too frequently admitted only the graduates of Ivy League and other "big name" colleges.

Herbert Brown, on the other hand, not only had good family connections with one of top management's members, but he had also just completed his education at the country's most prestigious graduate business school. So famous, it was merely known in business circles as "The School." Brown's M.B.A., naturally gave him a much higher starting salary than the others on the squad.

Both Green and Brown did well at Wilson's and upon the completion of the executive training program, they were both made assistant buyers in the men's and boys' wear division. Murray Green was assigned to the Boys' Furnishings Department and Herbert Brown to the Men's Sportswear Department.

After some time had passed, an opening occurred for an associate buyer in the Boys' Wear Department when Jack White who held that position left to take a buyer's job in Texas. The associate buyer's position in this instance had the responsibility for buying merchandise for the Boy Scout Shop, the Camp Shop, and boys' active sportswear.

Shortly after White's departure, an announcement was made by Ronald Black that Herbert Brown had been promoted to the associate buyer's vacancy. This news angered Murray Green who was secretly expecting the promotion himself. In the first place, he fumed, Brown is a real playboy—all show and no real work. Secondly, Murray had not only been working in the Boys' Department as an assistant buyer but he had had three years of part-time and summer vacation experience in the Boys' Department, including those seg-

135

ments covered by the associate buyer's duties. And finally, his ratings as an assistant buyer in that department were absolutely outstanding.

Murray Green sought an appointment with Ronald Black and pointed the above facts out to the divisional merchandise manager.

Black treated him most cordially and after listening to the obviously legitimate complaint, hastened to assure Murray Green, "You have a great future in the store, Murray. Don't you fret a bit. We've recognized for several years now that you're a great asset to Wilson's and we mean to take good care of you. As a matter of fact, see me next week because I think one of my plans for you may come to fruition by then."

Somewhat mollified, Murray Green went back to work and waited. Sure enough, without any prompting, the divisional merchandise manager called Murray into his office and told him of his promotion to department manager of men's and boys' wear at Wilson's newest and largest branch store. While this is in truth a promotion, because it provides more financial remuneration, there is also more travelling to the branch from his home—a real inconvenience. But what bothered Murray Green most was the fact that there were no buying responsibilities such as in the associate buyer's job that Herbert Brown had been promoted to. Murray's burning ambition was to get an opportunity to buy and he saw himself stymied at the branch store for at least two to four years before he could return to the main store as an associate buyer or a buyer.

Thus, while Murray Green accepted the promotion to branch store department manager, he became disenchanted with Wilson's. This disillusionment turned to fury when in a casual conversation with another department manager at the branch he made a startling discovery.

"Murray, I just can't believe you're that dumb," said Leonard White, "you've been working at Wilson's for about five years and it seems incredible to me that you didn't know you are knocking your brains out against the old crimson and black school tie. Unbelievable!"

"You mean that just because Herb Brown graduated from 'The School' he got that promotion?"

"And that's why he'll get the next buyer's job, too," continued White.

"Don't you know that your own merchandise manager, Ronald Black and the big guy, the general merchandise manager, Seymour Gelb, and of course, the president, Gray, and probably most of the other divisional merchandise managers and vice presidents all wear the same old school tie?"

"And to be someone at Wilson's," fumed Murray Green, "you have to have your M.B.A. from 'The School.' That's just great!"

This conversation gave Murray Green much food for thought. While he loved Wilson's—it was the only place he had ever worked —he despised its personnel policies insofar as his future was concerned. So, he made up a nice resume and sent some marked "Confidential" to a number of specialized employment agencies and executive search firms whose ads he had seen in *The New York Times* and in various trade papers. Murray was quite surprised and not a little pleased at the reaction to his resume at a number of these "head hunting" firms. On his day-off, he was interviewed in their offices and several made it clear that he would have no trouble at all as a buyer, but out-of-town—at distances away from New York. He soon learned that there was a great demand for people with a merchandising background and training such as his in cities outside New York.

One evening, the Gerard-Merrill Management Service, a leading merchandising consultant firm, with whom Murray Green had been in active contact, called him at home. They had a firm offer for him as a buyer of boys' wear with a very nice store in Corpus Christi, Texas. The store did about $15 million business annually and had a fine reputation in the community. The job provided an excellent salary and bonus arrangement, many fringe benefits, all relocation expenses paid and the agency's fee reimbursed. And to put the icing on the cake—practically a guarantee—that if he proved as good as his record, he would be a divisional merchandise manager in less than five years because of the store's retirement policies.

Murray Green put the phone down with his head spinning. He faced a real dilemma. His wife, Ruth, was a teacher in a local school system who had just been granted tenure; and her salary had given them more than a double income. Then, too, they both had their parents, family and many friends in the metropolitan area—Texas seemed so far away. Yet, Murray Green had seen his love for Wilson's destroyed by its favoritism in promotion.

What would you do if you were Murray Green?

Case 28
The Coverup

Richard Wilkens was the shoe buyer of McDonald's Department Store which was located in the eastern portion of the Midwest. Wilkens had been with the store for fifteen years and was considered a good buyer and "a solid citizen." In addition to his ability as a buyer, Wilkens was also recognized as a good trainer. Not only McDonald's but other stores had "graduates" of Wilkens' training who were now successful buyers.

Robert Collins was the current assistant buyer in McDonald's Shoe Department and he, too, literally worshipped the ground that Dick Wilkens walked on. Bob felt he owed his entire career to the great training he was receiving under Wilkens' tutelage. Unlike some buyers, Wilkens did not believe in holding back information or knowledge from his assistants. Thus, like all the other previous assistant shoe buyers, Bob Collins knew everything that was going on in the department. This was real on-the-job training, as it was meant to be.

Unfortunately, Dick Wilkens at this point in time was undergoing a series of bad personal experiences. First, his wife Nancy had a nervous breakdown and had to be confined to a local institution. Coincidentally, his oldest son Peter was caught in a drug raid and was in trouble with the law (Dick was too distraught to calculate which tragedy caused which to occur). And, as if he did not have enough troubles, Dick's sister Agnes called him from Jacksonville, Florida. Their eighty-six year old mother had become senile and Agnes needed Dick's help in getting her into a nursing home. Needless to say, all these personal problems necessitated Wilkens' absence frequently from the store. But, in Bob Collins, his assistant, he had not only a stalwart to lean on but a loyal friend to cover up for him if necessary. Incidentally, Dick Wilkens, who always relished his predinner cocktail, had begun drinking during this period in order to help him smooth over some of the rough spots, he thought.

During all the aforementioned troubles, Dick Wilkens was also trying to buy for the fall season. On one of the many days Wilkens was out of the store, Harry Best, the salesperson for Winchester Shoes, called on him. Winchester Shoes had been one of the department's key resources for many years and Harry Best was upset that the buyer was not available. This distress was heightened by the fact that in addition to the fall buying, Best had planned to offer the McDonald buyer a terrific close-out opportunity.

Being one of the department's principal suppliers, Harry Best took it upon himself to speak to John Gifford, the divisional merchandise manager, about the situation.

"John, you've got yourself a problem in your Shoe Department," Harry began. "We all know that Dick Wilkens is a top man, but he has been missing from the department more than he has been there these past weeks. That kid, Bob Collins, is terrific, and he will make one helluva buyer one of these years, but right now, he's in over his head, because Dick is always out."

Gifford shook his head slightly. "Harry, thanks for the tip. I owe you one for reminding me to look into the department—something I have been meaning to do for the past few weeks, but never got around to doing. You know, we divisional merchandise managers are primarily "figure" people and the figures for that department have been good—going ahead nicely. So, I guess I have been lulled. . . ."

Bob Collins, on the verge of exhaustion, towards the close of the next day received a call to see Gifford before he left the store.

When he had lowered himself into a seat, Gifford said, quietly, "Bob, I've done some extensive checking and you sure deserve a lot of credit, not to say praise. You've been carrying your department on your young shoulders almost single-handedly now for several months. Just answer one question for me, please. Where is Dick Wilkens and why isn't he here doing his job as buyer of your department?"

What should Bob Collins say?

Case 29
Sell! Sell! Sell!

Fred Marcus, the men's sportswear buyer of Brody's Department Store, which was located in a large Pacific Coast city, was going on his first long vacation in many years. Fred had arranged to take Georgette, his wife, on a three-week tour of the Orient, as a fifteenth wedding anniversary celebration. John Gross, the associate buyer of the department (who, incidentally, was number one on the general merchandise manager's list for promotion to buyer) was being given last-minute instructions by Fred Marcus.

John is a sharp person, highly motivated, well educated, and very articulate. He has been at Brody's for four years, starting out as an executive trainee. As the associate buyer of the Men's Sportswear Department, he is in nominal charge of selling activities, but also buys several segments of the department's merchandise including active sportswear, such as ski clothing. Everyone, including Fred Marcus, has full confidence in John's ability to handle the department during the buyer's absence.

"John, you have a relatively simple job," Fred Marcus was saying. "All you have to do while you're in charge is to sell. You have lots of merchandise, the racks are full. And your last big shipment is due on Monday. Your stocks are at peak."

"Don't worry, Fred, selling is my middle name," John replied assuredly.

"Of course, you can always put through a special order or two," Fred continued, "but otherwise, stay away from buying anything. We want to maintain our stock/sales relationship just as it is, and our stock turn for the period will come out just as we planned. Remember—the big word is SELL!"

With that, Fred Marcus left the department in John Gross' care. He was only gone a few days when Bill Walker, the sales manager of Todd & Todd, a nationally known branded merchandise company, came in to see Fred Marcus, unaware of his absence. Of course, he found John in charge. Bill knew John quite well since he had been buying ski wear and his firm made a well-known, nationally advertised line of ski clothing.

Bill Walker greeted John cordially but got down to business immediately. "John, I have a sensational offer for you of our Todd & Todd men's ski jackets in the latest colors and patterns and in a full size range. The jackets are our regular $100 retail sellers. I can give you a price on these jackets that will enable you to sell them for half price and you can still get your regular markup."

When John Gross inquired as to the reason for this great giveaway, Bill explained that Todd & Todd was having a temporary cash flow problem and that they had to convert a big part of their current stock to raise cash. To sweeten the pot, Bill Walker further offered to pay the entire cost of an ad in two major newspapers of Brody's Department Store's choice. These ads would enable the store to advertise truthfully that this nationally branded merchandise was being sold at 50% off.

Ernest Brenner, the divisional merchandise manager, listened attentively as John Gross laid out the Todd & Todd offer. While he was not too familiar with the exact merchandise, he did know the firm well.

"I'll say this to begin with, Jim," Brenner said, "I've known Todd & Todd for more than twenty-five years and everything they do or make is on the up-and-up. And I agree with your thinking that if we turn this down, one of our competitors will take it and scoop our market. So, if you feel this merchandise is salable, buy it. I'll approve the purchase order and get you the open-to-buy. But remember, I'm not telling you to buy it. You must use your own judgment."

Burning with the fervor of a possible great merchandising coup, John Gross bought the entire lot of three hundred ski jackets. The merchandise was delivered within twenty-four hours and the ads were rushed into print.

The promotion, despite the undeniable bargains offered, was one big failure, for no apparent reason other than apathy on the part of the buying public.

Fred Marcus returned from his trip to the Orient and he plunged right in to work, going over the department's records, reviewing what had occurred during his absence. Of course, he was able to put his finger on the problem immediately and he called John Gross into his office.

"John, you have made a serious error that is unforgivable for someone who is supposed to be a seasoned fashion merchandiser and who is allegedly ready to become a buyer."

What did Fred Marcus point out to John Gross?

DOLLAR PLANNING AND CONTROL— QUANTITATIVE PLANNING

THE NEED FOR PLANNING

The four "P's" of merchandising are: Planning, Purchasing, Promoting, and Profit. Proper planning can have a domino effect; if it is realistic and covers needs properly, it can be the means to profit. The planning process therefore is critical to the merchandising effort, particularly because the objective of all business efforts is profit. Desired results are achieved when the selling level is equal to, or better than, the planned volume and the stock in proper relationship to it (with adequate markup). It follows therefore that management has a high interest in the planning and control process to ensure proper stock investment and maximum return. Failure to plan properly can cause merchandise dislocations. The larger the organization, the greater dependency upon sophisticated planning.

The reasons for a dollar plan are:

1. To provide management with necessary data to cover capital requirements.
2. To help the buyer maintain a balance between sales and inventory.

DOLLAR PLANNING AND CONTROL RELATIONSHIP

The merchandise plan is a blueprint which includes: 1) a stock/ sales relationship; 2) merchandising standards.

Incorporated in the plan is a control feature that regulates the difference between planned stock and actual stock. During the period of actual performance, there are events that cause variations: sales, purchases, markdowns.

How these events cause variations will be discussed later in this chapter under "The Plan in Action."

The merchandise plan provides a resultant figure called *open-to-buy*—the budget a buyer can spend for merchandise for delivery within a given period.

PARTICIPANTS IN THE PLANNING

Obviously, the plan must be completed prior to the effective date of the plan's operation. How long a lead period is required depends upon the size, nature, and location of the operation.

The buyer always plays a part in the process, but the extent is dependent upon the type of organization. In a chain operation, the planner is the merchandise manager; in a department store, it is the buyer who either prepares the plan or contributes a major effort. In a department store or large specialty store, the plan starts with the buyer, is confirmed or worked out with the divisional merchandise manager, submitted to the general merchandise manager, and finally turned over to the controller or treasurer.

THE PLAN SEQUENCE

Information that will probably affect the merchandise activities of the period of the plan are made available to the planner by management so that the estimated sales figures can be projected most realistically. The information can be:

- Anticipated economic conditions
- Changes in competition
- Planned promotional efforts
- Changes in physical setup
- Changes in price line structure of the department

The budgeter then starts to work out a preliminary plan. The plan starts with the recording of the merchandising results of last year because it affords a framework of probability for the events that will happen during the period of the plan. Past records then are the levels that the merchandiser attempts to better, and the anticipated levels of achievement can be expressed in percentage figures. For example, if last year selling was $100,000, this year's goal could be $110,000 or 10% better.

A plan therefore is based on (1) experience and (2) anticipation.

The anticipatory factors, which are part of the buyer's expertise, include market strength and the probable customer acceptance level of merchandise offered for the selling season.

After weighing the completed preliminary plan, it is submitted to the next highest level of the organization for approval. It then becomes the dollar base around which a stock composition is built.

THE ELEMENTS OF A PLAN

The following are the essential figures:

1. Planned sales
2. Planned stock
3. Planned markdowns
4. Planned markup
5. Planned purchases

The related merchandising activity standards usually incorporated in a plan are:

1. Planned stock turnover
2. Planned cash discounts
3. Planned alteration costs
4. Planned selling costs
5. Planned advertising costs
6. Planned initial markup
7. Planned cumulative markup

The plan covers two periods: February through July and August through January.

The two most important figures are the planned sales and the planned inventory or stock.

PLANNED SALES

First last year's sales are recorded for the period; then the figures are recorded for each month. The next step is to estimate the sales for the period, and then for each of the six months. The estimates, as indicated in the previous section, are based on experience plus anticipation.

PLANNED STOCK

The amount of stock planned in relation to the planned sales is a management decision that is based on:

1. Past experience of the department
2. Norms or standards established by industry

The guidelines for the relationship between stock/sales:

1. Stock turnover
2. Stock/sales ratio

Stock turnover is an average figure for a period, calculated by dividing the average stock of a period (using the opening and closing inventory figures for the last month of the period) and dividing it into the sales for the period.

Stock/sales ratio is the retail stock as of a given date divided by the sales for the period it is used, usually for a month. The ratio is normally different for each month of the year.

It should be noted that estimates are in dollars and not, at this point concerned with units, assortments, or quantities of merchandise.

THE RETAIL INVENTORY SYSTEM

Most organizations use the retail inventory system which is based on recording all merchandise and merchandising activities at retail values.

The advantages are:

1. Ease of comparing figures with other stores.
2. Relatively efficient means of determining gross margin and net profit.
3. Ability to determine cost of merchandise (by application of a known percentage figure).
4. Ability to maintain close supervision of all merchandising functions.
5. Ease of determining the total dollar amount of stock on hand (book figure).

THE PLAN IN ACTION

Using Figure 5, follow the planning steps (for the month of February):

1. Last year's sales figures were filled in for the period.
2. Sales estimates were made for each month.
3. Planned sales were estimated on a stock/sales ratio of 2.
4. Retail purchases were calculated:

Planned sales–February	$ 3,300
Planned stock–EOM February	8,200
Planned markdowns–February	390
Total provision (or requirement)	$11,890
Less planned stock BOM February	−6,600
Planned retail purchases–February	$ 5,290

Note: Round figures are used because they are estimates; the ending inventory for February is the opening inventory for March.

THE CONTROL SYSTEM

Assume the date is March 1 and the buyer is planning the OTB for the month. Using Figure 5:

Planned sales	$ 4,100
Planned EOM stock (end of month)	7,200
Planned markdowns	500
Total provisions required	$11,800
Less planned inventory BOM	8,200
Planned retail purchases	$ 3,600
Stock variation (plus or minus)	−330
Total (unadjusted OTB)	$ 3,270
Less unfilled orders for delivery this month	700*
Open-to-buy this month	$ 2,570

The control feature is that the buyer was allowed $330 less than planned because the difference between the planned retail

---

* A compilation of orders placed with manufacturers taken from the buyer's file.

stock at March 1 and the actual stock on that date. This result was based on the February activities:

Planned sales–$3,300	Actual sales–$3,000	+ $300
Planned markdowns–$390	Actual markdowns–$370	+ 20
Planned retail purchases–$5,290	Actual retail purchases–$5,300	+ 10
		$330

These events caused the beginning of the month stock to be $330 more than anticipated. In a sense, the buyer is "penalized" for not achieving the goal and a brake was put on the amount of goods to be purchases—the control technique balances planned stock and sales.

THE MERCHANDISING STANDARDS (LEVELS OF ANTICIPATED ACHIEVEMENTS)

The plan commonly includes dollar or percentage figures related to or a percentage of net sales. They are: work room cost, cash discount, stock turnover, shortage, average stock, markdown, retail purchases, initial markup (the markon difference between costs and first retail prices), advertising, and gross margin. These are goals that are set to achieve a level of merchandising efficiency.

CONCLUSION

Profit is the result of careful planning. A plan is a guide and must be flexible and subject to change if conditions warrant.

A seasoned buyer can mentally calculate whether current events are consistent with the plan. In fact, an open-to-buy position can be taken for any period. For example, for a week or two weeks. In fashion merchandising, a buyer maintains a flexible position by not spending entire allotments; therefore being open, the buyer is in a position to purchase new market offerings.

If new market developments or stock needs occur, the buyer in a no-open-to-buy position must secure permission to exceed the levels of the plan from the merchandise manager. Whether permission is granted depends upon the need, the nature of the operation, and other factors.

What is of paramount importance is that the plan be realistic and used as a tool for maximum results.

	Department Name_____				Department No. _____			
						PLAN (This Year)	**ACTUAL** (Last Year)	
SIX MONTH MERCHANDISING PLAN	Workroom cost							
	Cash discount %							
	Season stock turnover							
	Shortage %							
	Average Stock							
	Markdown %							

SPRING 19— FALL 19		FEB. AUG.	MAR. SEP.	APR. OCT.	MAY NOV.	JUNE DEC.	JULY JAN.	SEASON TOTAL
SALES $	Last Year	3100	4000	3500	6000	5500	3700	24800
	Plan	3300	4100	3600	5100	6000	3940	26040
	Percent of Increase	6	3	3	2	9	7	5%
	Revised							
	Actual	3000						
RETAIL STOCK (BOM) $	Last Year	6000	8100	6900	9800	10,000	7200	
	Plan	6600*	8200	7200	10,200	12,200	8000	
	Revised							
	Actual	6600*	8530					
MARKDOWNS $	Last Year	420	567	450	828	791	501	
	Plan (dollars)	390	500	400	795	700	425	
	Plan (percent)							
	Revised							
	Actual	370						
RETAIL PURCHASES	Last Year	5620	3367	6850	6028	3491	3351	
	Plan	5290	3600	7000	7895	2600	3625	
	Revised							
	Actual	5300						
PERCENT OF INITIAL MARKON	Last Year							
	Plan							
	Revised							
	Actual							
ENDING STOCK	Last Year							6350
	Plan							7200
	Revised							
	Actual							

Comments

Merchandise Manager _____	Buyer _____
Controller _____	

*Comments — It is not realistic to assume that planned and actual figures will ever be the same. The use of identical figures are shown for the purpose of simplification at this point.

FIGURE 5 SIX MONTH MERCHANDISING PLAN

Case 30
The Planning Impasse

About four months ago, the Midwest Department Store in Sheboygan, Wisconsin, hired a new merchandise manager, Richard Thomas, who had a fine record at Marshall Field, Chicago. He was assigned to all the women's apparel departments.

The store had brought in merchandise consultants prior to hiring Thomas to determine ways to increase the ready-to-wear volume that was not up to comparable stores. The recommendations included the goal to increase the stock turn, which ranged from four to a little less than five times per year. This was below the standard of other stores in the region devoted to popular-priced merchandise. One of the strategies suggested was to set up an advertising program featuring specially priced merchandise.

Shortly after he arrived, Thomas held a meeting with the six buyers on his staff and outlined his plans.

He said, "We are shooting for a minimum stock turn of 6 times with a sales/stock ratio of 2 to 1. With additional advertising, thorough shopping of the market, and good vendor relations, we can make many good buys and pass them on to our customers. From here on we're going to make noise."

On July 14, Margery Porter, the accessories buyer, was with Thomas at the weekly buyer review meeting and presented her merchandise plan.

		Aug.	Sept.	Oct.	Nov.	Dec.	Jan.	Total
SALES	Ly (actual)	90,000	100,000	70,000	90,000	120,000	60,000	530,000
	Plan	99,000	110,000	80,000	99,000	132,000	66,000	586,000
RETAIL STOCK	Ly (actual)	225,000	250,000	175,000	225,000	300,000	150,000	1,325,000
	Plan	198,000	220,000	160,000	198,000	264,000	132,000	1,172,000

The merchandise manager scanned the plan and commented: "This form is OK, but the sales are increased 10% despite twice as many ads, improved displays and strong store programs. I'd judge that a 10% increase would be a poor record in view of the cost and efforts to stimulate real volume."

Margery was a little uptight. She did not approve of the hypodermic needle that the store was using, especially by Thomas, who she thought was overplaying the recommendations of the consulting firm. She defended her plan.

"A plan is a flexible tool. If conditions warrant increasing, open-to-buy, and a bullish approach, the plan can be changed. I can't see reasons for being unrealistic."

"Listen," Thomas responded, "modest increases indicate to management a lack of confidence, and poor psychology for you. I feel you won't be under sufficient pressure to top planned figures."

"Well," Margery retorted, "I submit high figures and leave myself vulnerable to downward revision and high markdowns. I'm going to look bad. Nothing doing, I don't want to play an unfair game, period."

Thomas was abashed. He did not expect this response from an outwardly calm young woman. Since his arrival, this was his first real encounter and he had not established a track record at the store. He was trying to win over the buyers and impress management. He simply could not afford an impasse at this early stage, the contingent results could do him no good.

What do you think should be Richard Thomas' course of action?

Case 31
A Fur Story

During the past two years, a strong customer trend for fur coats has developed. Many stores responded to the demand by stocking wide assortments of budget and better types of fur coats.

The Henry-Norman Department Store, an organization of one central city store and four suburban branches, has maintained a fur salon in the five stores. Since it is a family oriented operation featuring mostly popular merchandise, the fur department carries coats from $150 to $600, nothing too expensive.

Martin Saunders, the fur buyer, submitted his merchandise plan to his divisional merchandise manager yesterday. He was called into the merchandise manager's office this morning.

"Look here, Marty, your plan looks crazy," is how he was greeted. "The estimates are 25% over last year, in spite of a steady yearly increase of 10%. The 10% represents higher prices which is proven by the fact that the unit sales are about par with last year. Did your pencil slip, or did you latch on to a development that has escaped everyone?"

"No problem," Saunders replied. "I've decided to add a new classification, mink, at an average retail of $2,000. We can sell them easily. So my sales volume is assured, and this takes stock support. In fact, a 25% increase in sales is a conservative estimate."

"Marty, over my dead body. Perhaps you're right. Maybe we can sell mink coats, but do you realize what it will do to the department's figures? In the first place, the initial markup will suffer because you'll have to sell them at 20% markup. This will bring down the initial cumulative and maintained markup figures. In turn, it will affect the entire division. No sir, we aren't going in for it. I've got to make figures."

"Hold on," Marty cried, "do you mean to say you're going to hand the business over to our competition? Twenty percent may be the figure, but on a big ticket item we will sell more and make more."

"Not on your life. In a department store you are responsible for reaching standards, or bettering them, and I'm not falling for your arguments," stated the divisional merchandise manager emphatically.

The name of the game is profit, an adage the buyer knows well. But Martin Saunders is unable to comprehend the edict just handed down.

Weigh the facts and advise the buyer.

Case 32
Shooting Craps

Beverly Manners is the coat and suit buyer for Briton's Bargain Stores, Kankakie, Illinois. It is a hard-hitting organization that features merchandise at low prices. The store's slogan is *ABC—Always Better and Cheaper.*

Beverly was a department store buyer and is fully experienced in retail figures: she can plan, adjust, and achieve. One would have to recognize that she is a professional in every sense of the word.

Recently, she has been in a bind because of the unavailability of promotional merchandise suitable for the store's needs. The market has been depressed due to poor business, and manufacturers have cutback on production. The result is that few makers have disposable stock; the bargains have dried-up.

A few days ago, an old friend from the market, a manufacturer, called her long distance to advise her of a promotion that could perk up her business considerably. She was delighted and flew to New York to review the merchandise. She also planned to see fifteen to twenty manufacturers for possible future promotions.

She arrived in New York yesterday, and immediately visited Link Brothers, her friend's firm. Inspection of the coats, an overcut stock made for a larger mail-order firm, proved that they were indeed a bargain. Forty percent below original wholesale costs, fashionable, in suitable colors, and across the board in sizes.

A bonanza, she thought, just what the doctor ordered. One problem, Link will sell the goods on the condition that we purchase the entire lot of twenty-five hundred garments. A lot of merchandise, she mused, but in the middle of the season they will sell with a short markup. The store needs the business, and this group can bring heavy traffic.

That evening she called Artie Lang, the president of Briton's, and outlined the details. He was impressed with Beverly's intensity and desire to perk up business but he had strong doubts.

"In the first place," he said, "twenty-five hundred coats are an awful lot of garments and a big investment of $50,000. Second, business is poor and your actual B.O.M. stock is 15% over your plan. Finally, if the sale is a dud and there is no such thing as a sure winner, you'll be in the soup. Can't you talk Link into partial purchase with an option to buy the remainder? We can run a fast sale and establish a rate of sale; then unload them if we're successful. He's your friend, press him."

"I've tried it," she replied. "I've tried every gimmick in the book. He's anxious to sell, but he knows he can get rid of the goods in one shipment to any number of stores. He called me first out of friendship."

"Beverly, I love you, but good business practice dictates that one doesn't shoot craps. You are overbought and don't have a dime of open-to-buy."

"If I had open-to-buy money, I wouldn't call you in the first place," she retorted.

"Sorry," he said.

Beverly is depressed. She has the chance to buy perfect merchandise, which could be a lifesaver. She knows her store's stock position, but feels it could be reduced with a successful ad. That darn merchandise plan, does one have to live and die by it, she thought.

Beverly being a fighter does not give up easily. She prevailed on Link to give her a twenty-four hour option on the promotion, promising to call after returning home. She is on the plane and planning a strong case to overcome her bosses' objections.

If you were Beverly Manners, plan an approach you feel will open a budget for the purchase.

Case 33
The Inexperienced
Buyer

You are the ladies' sportswear buyer for Culver Fashions, Culver City, California. It is July and you are about to submit a six month (August thru January) merchandise plan for your department.

You have reviewed the events of last year and remembered that the weather in August and September was most unfavorable for selling. The heat was constant and caused consumer lassitude. Your figures for the two month period were off about 18%. You recall worrying yourself sick to make figures.

This year you visited the market in June for fall merchandise and were not impressed with the trends. Although you have been a buyer for only a year, you believe a one color trend, grey heather, may spell trouble. Accordingly, you bought merchandise well below your budgeted figures. You are in a strong open-to-buy position, and very liquid.

Your one worry is that it is not reasonable to assume that business will be adversely affected to the extent of last year. Lightning cannot strike twice. If the market shows real strength, you could plan a strong increase of sales for the two opening months of the plan with some scrambling. Because you are new, you feel you are between the devil and deep blue sea. If you plan for a decrease it may be considered as a defensive measure by a new buyer. Should you plan unrealized figures, you could be strongly criticized and look like an inefficient new buyer.

You consider going to your merchandise manager and laying the cards on the table. He is a fine man, but he has some misgivings about you being a buyer. He feels you lack experience, actually, he hired you after considerable soul searching. Therefore you discard the idea.

The other ready-to-wear buyers are bullish, but they don't have the same trouble. They suffered losses last year, but they have affirmative feelings about the opportunities for increases this year. Business, this year, they maintain must be better than last year's disaster.

What are you going to do?

XII

MERCHANDISE ASSORTMENT PLANNING— QUALITATIVE PLANNING

The composition of the merchandise that is offered to the clientele of a store is part of the retail marketing strategy. It is management's responsibility to target a market group. It is the buyer's responsibility to select the "what" that will accommodate the needs and wants of that segmented group. The philosophies of assortment, depth, price ranges, price zones, peak stock dates, and other important stock characteristics are set by management. It is the buyer's assignment to build a stock condition within the framework of guidelines established by top echelon of the retail organization.

The buyer has sources of information that are used to round out an adequate stock condition that is consistent with management's goals and customer wants. Here are sources for a buyer's guidance:

STORE POLICIES

A policy is a governing principle, plan or course of action. Management lays down a set of principles that will determine the direction within which a stock will be built as part of the appeals for customer patronage.

These are among the most common principles:

1. *National Brands*—the decision to stock customer-identified merchandise from nationally known resources.
2. *Exclusivity of Merchandise*—the possible need to secure some competitive advantage by having merchandise not available to competing stores; for a part of a line or period of time, or some arrangement that makes the store headquarters in the trading area for specific merchandise.
3. *Pricing*—an appeal to high income people demands merchandise at better priced levels. Conversely, low income customer levels require promotionally priced goods.
4. *Sales Promotion Factors*—how a store communicates with its customers and therefore, how it educates and sells goods is another market strategy. When and how promotional events are planned are included in the tactics utilized to influence the selected market.
5. *Service Factors*—this part of the marketing mix affects the buyer's plans to the extent that there is awareness that certain goods require sales help as an efficient, or necessary, condition of selling.
6. *Mail-Order Policies*—a mail or telephone order program requires merchandise that has sufficient appeal to be accepted by the customer when it is seen first at home. Merchandise specification, quantity preparation, back-up merchandise, and realistic advertising are part of the buyer's concern.

CUSTOMER CHARACTERISTICS

A merchant must study the cross-section of the population to which the store makes its appeals. The broader the population the more complex the "problems," particularly because different customers have different definitions of the meaning of fashion.

The statistical data about customer groups (demographics) are easily obtained and understood. The difficult responsibility is what makes for attitudes, opinions, and beliefs (psychographics).

Some important general customer likes and dislikes include:

1. Most customers want sufficient stock on hand to make comparisons.

2. Older customers want merchandise developed to enhance their appearances, such as, short and long sleeves (to hide wrinkles), necklines that cover signs of age.
3. Certain European ethnic groups buy wedding dresses at high prices, above what income levels would dictate.
4. Lower income groups tend to favor high shades. High income groups favor more subtle shades.
5. Young people are prone to accept newness earliest.
6. Men prefer specialty shops. Women buy a substantial percentage of men's furnishings.
7. Brand importance varies with groups and nature of the merchandise.
8. Customers dislike fashions that are "knocked off"* easily and become "fords"** shortly after purchase.
9. The purchase of fashion is based on enhancement, or a state of betterment.
10. Customers are generally agreed that present quality standards are too low (even at better price levels).
11. Customers resent being forced to buy fashion long before end use; a condition based on the market's practice to accommodate its own needs.
12. Insufficient stock to support promotional events is strongly disliked by all customers.
13. Classic merchandise is expected to be available in sufficient quantity for customer choice.
14. Customers resent lack of coordination among the fashion departments. For example, dress departments should stock styles in prices, colors, silhouettes, and details that accommodate purchases in coat, sportswear, and suit departments.
15. Above all, customer patronage is best served when the customer is comfortable, which includes a stock condition that reflects what a customers should reasonably expect.

ESTABLISHED CUSTOMER BUYING PATTERNS

Customers follow certain patterns of buying which, of course, are known to the buyer. Stock size is, therefore, at a high level before

---

* "Knock off" is the common practice of copying a higher priced garment.
** "Ford" is a very popular style available from many manufacturers at different prices simultaneously.

strong demand and is reduced to low levels when customer demand is weakest.

The customer calendar includes the following conditions:

1. January is clearance month.
2. Heaviest spring buying precedes Easter.
3. Post-Easter is usually the spring clearance period.
4. Post-Easter is often the start of summer.
5. July is the promotional month for summer goods.
6. The day after July 4 is fall.
7. August and September are the strong selling months of fall.
8. October is a clearance month.
9. December is the store's highest volume month; and departments selling suitable gift merchandise are at peak selling levels.
10. Other traditional promotions are exemplified by: Mother's Day, Father's Day.

MERCHANDISE TIMING

When merchandise is offered to customers was discussed in Chapter II in the unit, "The Evolutionary Character of Fashion." Although many changes have taken place in the value system of Americans and what is really suitable fashion, the one practice that has remained is that highest priced merchandise is bought and featured earliest. Customers for expensive fashions expect newness early.

An added consideration is that store location will dictate stock peak dates. Some New York department stores tend to defer widest fall assortments, for example, until August 15. Lower California stores have learned that September can bring temperatures over one hundred degrees; and, therefore, extend summer by continuing to feature lightweight clothing. On the other hands, stores in the Boston area can extend winter selling later than many parts of the country.

It might be said that timing depends upon:

1. The customer group (size and nature)
2. The price levels and market segment
3. The location of the store
4. Regional characteristics (some areas are slow to acceptance)

INTERNAL SOURCES OF INFORMATION

The store is where it all takes place. There are numerous sources of information for the alert buyer to build a fund of knowledge:

1. Salespeople
2. Floor observation
3. Sales records (to be discussed separately in this chapter)
4. Want slips
5. Trends in related departments
6. Customer surveys
7. Customer panels
8. Fashion shows
9. Fashion coordinator

EXTERNAL SOURCES OF INFORMATION

The buyer is offered almost an unlimited means of determining what customers will probably want. The following is a list of areas easily accessible:

1. The resident buying office
2. Advisory fashion consultants (arranged by the store)
3. Fashion magazines
4. Manufacturers
5. Trade publications
6. Textile market
7. Data from competing and noncompeting stores
8. Newspapers
9. Television and motion pictures
10. Observing people

TECHNIQUES OF PLANNING AND CONTROL OF ASSORTMENTS

UNIT CONTROL
(THE PERPETUAL INVENTORY SYSTEM)

One of the most useful tools for merchandising is a unit control system. This important source of information avails the buyer information of past and current customer preferences. By definition it is a recording system that shows the movement of specific merchandise. The system provides a record of the following in numbers of units:

- Price lines
- Colors
- Classification
- Styles
- Vendors
- Purchases
- Sales
- Any other desired information

It is really not a control system in the strictest sense; the buyer is able to secure precise information and then exercise some form of control (buy more, markdown to clear out, promote, etc.). The course of action to be taken is a matter of buyer judgment.

The system used in fashion merchandising to obtain the information discussed is called the *perpetual inventory system.* The system provides for a record of the movement of every piece of merchandise—from the time it is received by the store until it is sent to the customer. It can be maintained manually or by electronic data processing.

The perpetual inventory system is a means of helping the buyer achieve a balance between sales and merchandise in terms of units—the specifics—the "what."

The system can be tailored to show the movement by price levels, manufacturers, silhouette, fabrics, colors, or any desired compilation of data that is useful for the buyer.

The most practical advantages are that it:

1. Reveals best selling styles and therefore, records customer preferences.
2. Also reveals poor selling merchandise.
3. Offers a wide variety of information that can be seen easily.
4. Affords analysis for future merchandising decisions.
5. Shows the inventory level of merchandise on hand for sale.

The disadvantages are that it is:

1. Costly
2. Subject to human error

CLASSIFICATION MERCHANDISING

As a further help to a buyer, a classification system is incorporated in the planning process. This activity is a method of establishing units of customer demands, one that couples any one or combination of end use requirements into one class. For examples, sweaters are a unit of customer demand. This is a broad classification, probably too broad for an active selling group of merchandise. Hence, a further refinement can be made by establishing subclassifications: Long sleeve crew necks, long sleeve turtle necks, etc. This would permit more specific analysis and stock investment.

This system allows for:

1. The ability to plan stock/sale, ratio with greater accuracy.
2. The development of a practical open-to-buy position.
3. The evaluation of narrow segments of merchandise.
4. The spotting of trends.
5. The avoidance of duplication of goods.

Fashion merchandise can change dramatically; therefore, subclassifications must be flexible, eliminated or added as circumstances warrant based on new market offerings and customer preferences.

It is evident that the fashion buyer does not work in a vacuum. A professional buyer is a people-watcher, but also one who has almost unlimited sources of information from which to cull market offerings and build an assortment of merchandise for the customers of the store. Hence, an open mind, the ability to get along with people, and the application of what is available, are all part of the characteristics needed for successful buying.

Case 34
To Brand or
Not To Brand

Bruce Gregory is the recently hired buyer of men's furnishings on the main floor of Jones Department Store, Philadelphia, Pennsylvania. The store's volume is over $50 million a year. The Men's Furnishings Department, as is the case in all major stores, is a well-developed, well-trafficked section.

Bruce has been studying the operation with extreme care. Not only because he is new, but also because he has been advised that he is going to be called upon to make several important merchandising decisions. Bruce had been a men's furnishings buyer in a major store in New York City and was up-to-date on market developments.

One of the aspects that surprised Bruce is the dominance of brand names. Practically all merchandise stocked is from nationally known makers. When this fact came to his attention, he spoke to several of the salespeople. Their remarks indicated that the store's policy favored heavy concentration on labels, and that most of the brands had been carried for many years. He learned that the customers seemed to prefer brand names, as indicated by a continuous department growth. However, he also learned that on many occasions Jones' had been scooped by other stores because new styling was not available from their larger size resources. He recognized that overbranding can be inhibitive—shutting the door to new creativity. He studied the classifications and could readily see that at least six items that deserved to be included in stock were absent.

Now he knew that he had to take a stand. He realized that the department functions well, but is it obtaining potential? Another disturbing element is that the store has shut itself off from the market. As a buyer, he concluded, he would have a selection of merchandise offering of relatively few resources. His associations will be of no real value, and from a selfish point of view, he would lose all his meaningful contacts. Besides, he wondered, how long before customers recognize that the store is standing pat in a new, exciting market.

Bruce is concerned. The aphorism that a new broom sweeps clean is very much in his mind. He does not want to confront his superior because logically he would conjecture:

- You are new and do not understand the operation.
- Which resources would you discard?
- Our customers depend upon specific brands, to a large degree they mean customer patronage.

He is aware that he cannot make a presentation without data that proves his thesis, "It is possible to be overbranded."

What steps would you recommend to Bruce Gregory, and how would you present your findings to management?

Case 35
You Can't Win
Them All

The largest retail operation in the state of Colorado is Bon Ton, a ten unit chain of department stores. Their customer group represents a wide spectrum of customers, ranging in family income from $8,000 to $40,000 per annum. Consequently, the assortment of merchandise offered is extremely wide and deep.

At the end of the last fiscal period, management was concerned about the increasing markdown rate in the ready-to-wear departments. They interviewed fashion buyers who agreed that the wide assortments made the departments vulnerable to price reductions.

At a meeting involving all the fashion apparel buyers, it was announced that a new program would be followed to cut down on classifications. Wherever possible, minimum stock would be carried for items that did not justify wide customer choices. Unit control records were to be examined, rate of sale reviewed, and buyer judgment for each segment's value to be established. On that basis, future investments would be made.

Susan Evers, the shoe buyer, did her homework. Her study disclosed that several classifications were carried for the convenience of a small number of customers, and if one considered the tie-up of capital, they were maintained at a loss. Subsequently, the categories of loafers, basic pumps, and oxford styles were marked down and cleared out of stock.

After a short period of time, salespeoples' Want Slips listed all three styles, particularly oxfords. Evers noted the information and followed through by spending time on the selling floor to obtain information firsthand. The research proved what she suspected. Older customers, fifty-five years and over, were requesting the no longer stocked merchandise. On two occasions, the customers complained that the store favored the young and was insensitive to loyal customer needs, and that the articles could be purchased at competitors.

She studied past records again to reinforce her decision. No matter how she worked the figures, the three classifications were the least important. She felt badly, but store policy had to guide stock composition.

Then the calamity. A disgruntled customer wrote a letter to the editor of the local newspaper complaining about the world's concern for the young and the disregard for the old. The example given was the elimination of styles in the Shoe Department of Bon Ton.

The president of the store, Gilbert Hughes, asked Evers for a detailed report. Evers submitted the report and waited to see Hughes in his office.

Without ado, he proceeded to give her a lesson in merchandising with the theme, "The customer is always right, and merchandise is stocked for customers."

She was horrified. She was being castigated for a store policy to eliminate non-productive categories. If she was financially secure, she would have quit the job on the spot. Discretion caused her to keep a tight-lip and say nothing.

The meeting took place last Thursday, and it is now Saturday night. Evers is reflecting about the incident and wants to take some action that will express her point of view without putting herself in a bad light.

If you were Susan Evers, what would you do?

Case 36
Who are the Customers?

A meeting was in progress in The Sample, one of the oldest stores in New York City, founded in 1820. The president, Roy Stephans, was addressing the staff.

"This is probably the most critical meeting ever held. The outcome might spell the difference between success and failure. Despite a long history, a prime Fifth Avenue location, and a cooperative management organization, we are losing our share of the market. Simply put, we are losing customers, profit, and possibly the store itself.

"As you know, in our enviable history we have had customers of the highest stations and income. Our Dress Department is nationally known for innovative styles as well as its relationships with top designers. Our Beauty Salon still caters to famous people who must make appointments in advance.

"We are simply not offering and selling the right merchandise, and drastic steps must be taken to affect changes to turn the situation around."

Each merchandise manager then held a departmental meeting. Bruce Nevins, the ready-to-wear divisional merchandise manager, proposed that each of his buyers take one important classification and analyze it.

His instructions were: "Head the sheet with the classification description, list the price levels, and rate each level in order of importance. In a separate column, re-evaluate the classification to its department's contribution and then restructure each price level in order of importance, based on your interpretation of customers we should be selling.

"I want relevancy to the statistics, demographics of the population of New York City. Certainly there has been dramatic changes during the past ten years. Your report should include customer attitudes about The Sample and the stock we presently offer. Of course, your evaluation should include reasons why recommended new price lines and merchandise types should sell to the new targeted group."

You are the ladies' sportswear buyer and have selected sweaters as the subject of your research. Your present classification breaks down as follows:

		Priority
$75	Cashmere cardigan	5
$60	Cashmere long sleeve slip-on	1
$50	Cashmere short sleeve slip-on (novelty)	2
$40	Fine gauge wool cardigan	3
$30	Fine gauge wool long sleeve slip-on	4
$20	Orlon cardigan	6
$15	Ban-lon sleeveless, mock turtleneck	7

You are the buyer's assistant and have been asked to submit a report which your department manager will use as a comparative point of view. You know that you can obtain the necessary demographics from the library and you are not worried about submitting a creditable report. You know New Yorkers; where they live; how they live; their incomes; their life styles. In fact, you know the New York stores that do a good job—and why. Backup your conclusions with supportive data.

SELECTION OF RESOURCES

The purchase of merchandise is one of the most important functions of a buyer. It is one area of merchandising that is the responsibility of *all* buyers, whether they are complete merchants or market specialists. Therefore the selection of those resources that are best suited for the needs of the customers of an organization is an important buyer consideration.

For what purpose, when and how often a market trip is made, depends upon the nature, location, and policies of an operation.

The most important fashion market is located in New York City; but other areas exist in Rochester, Los Angeles, Dallas, Boston, Philadelphia. Since World War II, stores have used foreign markets located in Europe and the Orient, and in the middle seventies, South America.

ADVANTAGES OF BUYING FROM DOMESTIC MANUFACTURERS VS. FOREIGN MANUFACTURERS (or from representatives operating from the United States)

Since there are about twenty-five thousand U.S. fashion apparel manufacturers, there must be advantages to their being used. These domestic suppliers offer:

1. Delivery terms
2. Proven merchandise specifications
3. Close manufacturer relationships
4. Availability of reorders

5. Availability of selected quantities
6. Responsibility for merchandise received
7. Opportunity to test rate of sale
8. Opportunity to evaluate line importance to a total market
9. Ease of planning and controlling stock
10. Stock adjustment to new trends

On the other hand, there are advantages in using foreign resources:

1. Lower prices for promotional minded stores.
2. Availability of resources for mass distributors that have restraints placed on them by certain U.S. companies.
3. Availability of merchandise having characteristics not obtainable in U.S.
4. Opportunities for specification merchandising, making for higher markup.
5. Some foreign merchandise are status symbols.
6. Retail opportunity to offer a wider variety of merchandise.

METHODS OF OBTAINING IMPORTS

The simplest way to obtain foreign goods is to buy from an importer with stock goods in the United States.

The obvious advantages are:

1. Limited transportation costs.
2. Shorter delivery terms.
3. Greater responsibility for delivered merchandise.

The disadvantages are:

1. Availability of merchandise to competition.
2. Competition eliminates ability to obtain higher markup.

The disadvantages to using foreign markets include:

1. The absence of the buyer from the store.
2. The cost of transportation, accommodations, and other personal expenses.
3. Requirement for long-term commitments.
4. Buyer responsibility for size specifications of garments.
5. Buyer responsibility for fashion prediction.
6. New competitive factors among U.S. stores in use of foreign markets, which have tended to drive costs up.

7. Responsibility of risks usually assumed by a domestic manufacturer.

BUYER SOURCES OF INFORMATION FOR SELECTION OF RESOURCES

Although this subject would seem to be one that would be best known only to the seasoned experts, it is far from the truth. Actually, the information is easily obtained; the difficulty is the judgment needed to build and maintain a relationship with those sources that can best accommodate the needs of a department.

Following is a list of sources from which the right manufacturers can be obtained.

1. Resident buying office
2. Competing stores
3. Other buyers
4. Market centers (including regional markets)
5. Trade advertising
6. Trade directories
7. Observation at events (including fashion shows)
8. Want Slips from sales personnel (intra-store)

CRITERIA FOR SELECTION OF RESOURCES

This unit concentrates on the selection of new resources not used by the store, since active makers are evaluated on the basis of their record of store contribution.

The buyer therefore uses all or some combination of the following criteria.

APPROPRIATENESS OF MERCHANDISE

All merchandise in stock must have a level of importance to customers. The importance is related to the nature of the operation, to whom the appeal is being made, as discussed in Chapter II.

DISTRIBUTION POLICY OF MANUFACTURERS

Every manufacturer selects channels of distribution (stores) that can achieve marketing objectives. The store has its marketing objectives, among which is a policy of the type of competition it wishes to face. Therefore the competitive factor that a manufacturer sets up by reason of what stores will be sold in the trading area is a primary concern of the buyer and management. One of the first questions a buyer will ask the manufacturer is "Who do you sell in my area?"

TIMING

A manufacturer delivers ties-in with one of, or a combination of, the following needs: fashion newness, required stock peaks, promotional events, reorders. The manufacturer gears his delivery based on what types of stores fit into his marketing strategy.

SPECIFICATIONS

How a garment fits depends upon the garment specifications of the maker. As a rule of thumb, better-priced manufacturers specifications are more liberal than those of popular-priced makers because of the cost of the fabric. It is the buyer's responsibility to determine whether the manufacturer's specifications are those that are suitable for the customers of the department.

RETAIL PRICE MAINTENANCE

Price maintaining stores avoid competition that feeds on short markups, or marks goods down opportunistically. One of the major reasons for dropping a resource is unfair practices by competing stores. The manufacturer must have some control over the retail prices of stores he services to ensure fair competition. Since manufacturer price maintenance power can be practiced only when the sale rate of merchandise is satisfactory, the buyer must select successful resources.

CLEARANCE POLICIES

The buyer is aware that at some point the maker will have merchandise that must be disposed of at close-out levels. Someone, somewhere, is going to "sale"* the merchandise. The buyer, again, may face the contingency of unfair conditions. Leading questions that will be posed are: "When do you sell off-price merchandise? To whom? At what price levels?"

---

* Promote at less than original retail prices.

DELIVERY POLICIES

A store cannot sell from empty shelves, "milk" a style with poor reorder delivery, or maintain a competitive level, if deliveries do not support required stock positions. This is an area of constant buyer awareness. There is further recognition that a manufacturer's delivery often reflects his attitude about the store's importance. Broken stock deliveries, for example, are not appreciated by all buyers, and not accepted by chain stores.

ADVERTISING POLICIES

Although a buyer's concern is appropriate merchandise, there is always the thought that cooperative advertising is valuable. Co-op money is in reality a cost reduction. Above all, the buyer must buy merchandise, not advertising, which if available, is a plus factor. Manufacturers' national advertising is a means of establishing brand identification and can be an added advantage, if that feature is part of the policy of the store.

PRICES AND TERMS

Showroom prices as a trade practice remain firm. Only at the end of a season or when poor selling dictates, are the prices and terms subject to revision to lower levels. Advantageous terms are often obtainable as a condition of sale and as a means to enhance departmental profits.

BRAND IDENTIFICATION

Brand identification is part of the policy of the store. It is a matter that requires discussion with and approval of the merchandise manager.

CONCLUSION

These factors are weighed and are the basis of resource selection. The determination must include the buyer realization that the resource must afford all or in part: consumer appropriateness and compatibility with store policies; resource growth potential; merchandise availability and competitive competition; profitability.

CLASSIFICATION OF RESOURCES

Resources are means of maintaining the main ingredient of retailing and therefore, their importance is graded and defined by type:

1. A *key* resource is profitable, character building for the department, and used season after season.
2. *Stock* resource is a supplier used fairly consistently.
3. *Item* resource is used for specific styles or events.
4. *Classification* resource is a specialist in a given classification of merchandise.
5. *Secondary* resource is used from time to time.
6. *Shopping* resource is worthy of shopping and possibly used in the future.

CONCENTRATION ON RESOURCES

Benefits most often accrue from close relationships. Hence, a store attempts to develop and maintain a number of such arrangements. In the long run, the following benefits may be available:

1. Markdown money for poor selling styles (a practice manufacturers try to avoid).
2. Return of poor selling styles (sometimes).
3. Manufacturer fashion shows in store (trunk showings).
4. Inducements for salespeople (P.M.'s).
5. Interior displays (supplied by the manufacturer and used if in line with policy).
6. Exclusivity of merchandise (including specification merchandise, if desired).
7. Preferred delivery (initial and reorder).
8. Co-op ad money, if available.

However, the following are a few possible disadvantages which may sometimes mar a close relationship, more often when the maker is confident of his strength with the store; but not infrequently, when the buyer incorrectly assesses the manufacturer's motives.

1. Delivery of merchandise not as ordered (styles, quantities, sizes, etc.).
2. Setting up new competition (selling another store).

In addition, buyer's lethargy can result in the omission of deserving newcomers—new makers with new important lines.

CONCLUSION

There is no mystery about where merchandise can be purchased—there are more vendors than can be used. It is the buyer's assignment and responsibility to seek, evaluate, select, develop, and maintain resources to achieve a stock position desirable for the customers of the retail organization.

The type of store and its strategies will dictate:

1. The number of resources needed
2. The use of foreign markets
3. Which brands are maintained
4. Whether fashion leadership is exercised
5. The required quality levels
6. When merchandise is delivered
7. The extent of concentation on resources
8. The resource price levels

Case 37
You're Only Young Once

Sue Grapper is the new lingerie buyer of Poor's, one of the major department stores in Detroit, Michigan. Her appointment followed three and a half years experience as an assistant buyer.

She is in New York on her first market trip and is deeply impressed with the tempo of the market and concerned with the responsibility of her new job. While at the resident buying office on Monday, her first day in New York, the representative, Mary Todd, recommended a resource not carried by the store.

"LeMay is one of the hottest houses in the market. They have a designer who has a golden touch. They produce their own goods and advertise well. You can't afford to be without them."

A visit to the resource proved that the resident buying office buyer was right. The styles are exciting, the new colors are exquisite and the delivery schedule satisfies Sue's needs.

Sue made the appropriate notes for later order placement. However, before leaving she asked the salesperson about the firm's distribution in the Detroit area.

"Oh," he said, "we sell everybody. In fact, the state of Michigan is our best volume producer."

Sue mentioned several competitors and learned that all are strong LeMay users.

"Do any of the stores have promotional plans," she queried.

"Let me look up our records and I'll let you know."

Sure enough, the whole town seemed bent on advertising the same styles.

The next morning, with her notes in hand, she visited the resident office and related the story to her representative.

"Mary, every 'drug' store has the goods and plans on advertising them. If I buy the goods for stock, I'll have a limited assortment in comparison with my competition. More than that, any company that sells every store in town must be in trouble sooner or later. Somebody is going to break prices, and then everybody will do the same. I just don't like the idea."

The representative advised, "No one can be without the hottest house in town. What will you say to your customers when they ask for the goods; and what will you say to your bosses when they see the ads?"

Sue responded, "Well, the customers will be able to buy the

merchandise at Army/Navy and discount stores, they won't ask or need us."

"Not this season," replied Mary. "Not the way they're selling goods. No one is going to break prices when a resource is hot and jeopardize reorder delivery."

"Well," Sue responded, "I'll speak to my divisional merchandise manager and recommend that we pass up LeMay despite their success. I don't intend to buy from a house whose distribution policy is to sell everybody."

What is your opinion of the action Sue Grapper has taken? Keep in mind that she is a new buyer on her first market trip, the selling rate justifies "purchase," and her credibility as a professional has not been established in the eyes of her superiors.

Case 38
When It Rains,
It Pours

Meirs and Cent is one of the largest retailers in the United States. They operate eight hundred and fifty department stores and a huge mail-order business, about 15% of a volume of $5 billion a year.

The Children's Sweater Department is merchandised on the basis of a Listing and Price Agreement Plan. The buyer commits the parent organization to a quantity of goods that should suffice the stores' needs for a given period. The manufacturer finishes the goods and drop ships all orders. Under the plan, a store has the discretion of ordering or disregarding the home office bulletins. It gives autonomy and responsibility to each store. The home office is responsible to the manufacturer for the stock. Stores are billed at a "loaded" price. The "load" is a small profit for the office to offset inventory losses.

Chris Brandon, the children's sweater buyer, although highly motivated is also insecure. His limited experience as a buyer, three years, and his family, a wife and two children, weigh heavily on him.

During January of this year, he committed for twelve thousand dozen of an orlon cardigan with Grey Knitting Mills, at $45 a dozen. For reasons he could not fathom, the season ended with twenty-seven hundred dozen garments in the manufacturer's warehouse. Ben Siegal, a principal of Grey, started to dun Chris to move the goods. Chris offered the sweaters to the stores at a reduced price after the season, with no takers.

In reviewing plans with Jim Delaney, the merchandise manager, Chris referred obliquely but not specifically to the sweater stock at Grey. He took for granted that since the merchandise is classic, an order for the next year in January would detail the same style, in new colors, and in quantities to balance those on hand. An order for about five or six thousand dozen, on the light side, would get him out from under and relieve the tension. Neither man wanted to own up to the miscalculation and have it a matter of record.* They thought orders for the next year would eliminate the liability.

---

* Actually, Jim was completely aware of the stock condition. He had been in the similar situation before and was able to have a buyer fill in and dispose of the carried over goods.

As luck would have it, his merchandise manager was assigned to a new position in California, and the replacement was a tough, rigid divisional manager from another section. Chris knows the man's reputation and is concerned. He thought, he would get an order signed before Jim Delaney leaves and be in the clear. He could not afford to get Jim or himself in trouble with the new broom. However, Delaney had to leave for his new assignment before Chris could reach him.*

But "when it rains, it pours." Last week, Ronald L. Evers, the new general merchandise manager, called Chris into his office and related the following.

During a trip to Puerto Rico, he met the two partners of Stonehenge Knitting Mills, an organization with complete, up-to-date mill facilities on the island. The machinery included James high speed machines that produce fine gauge garments of the highest quality; finished products comparable to Grey's garments at $36 a dozen.

Chris started to sweat when he heard Evers say, "Chris, the resource is located at 1407 Broadway, call them and make a date to shop the line. I'll be interested in your evaluation of the line and how it stocks up against Grey. We haven't made a commitment for next year, have we?"

"No, we haven't."

Oh boy! thought Chris.

He called Stonehenge, spoke to one of the partners and went to their office. Despite his desire to find fault with the merchandise, Chris had to admit that the quality and value were far superior to his deal with Grey.

How was he going to get out of the predicament? His firm owned a stock of over twenty-five hundred dozen that could not be shipped without an additional fill-in order.

Also, how can he commit for the sweater in face of a competitive sweater that is cheaper and better? The new resource deserves his business. They pass every standard set up by Meirs and Cent.

Chris Brandon needs a friend, and advice. Can you explain his alternatives?

---

* In a big organization both divisional and general merchandise managers were reassigned.

Case 39
The Merchandise by
Any Other Label. . . .

One of the hottest houses in the New York market is KICKS, a junior size manufacturer that is "in." Their styling is casual, young, and a symbol of being "with it" for high school and college students. *"If you do not have a KICK, you are out."*

The company is owned by two relatively young men who were ready-to-wear buyers for Macy's. It is apparent that they know the business. Part of their business philosophy is to sell price maintaining stores which they rigidly enforce. Price cutters are removed from their roster of accounts.

This level of success has continued from the day they started business five years ago. Some stores, impressed with the acumen and record of the maker, have opened "Kicks Korner Shops," a strategy suggested by the maker.

Main Street, the largest department store chain of California, is one of the biggest users of KICKS, in the vernacular, they virtually barrel goods out.

One store policy concerning resource criterion is that Main Street will never share a resource with a discount store within their trading area.

Two weeks ago, a comparison shopper for Main Street reported that The Mart, a twenty-six store discount chain, carries KICKS. A customer complaint involving a jean priced at $4 less at The Mart was the reason for the investigation.

Carol Baker, the buyer, called KICKS long distance collect.

"Listen," she explained, "we do a great job. I can't understand how you can ship to a discounter and hurt us. It doesn't make sense, particularly since you're familiar with our store policy. Profitable operation or not, management looks at the long-term meaning to customers. They'll refuse to allow me to carry your goods."

Ben Gardner, a partner, explained, "Don't get excited, Carol. We don't ship The Mart any part of our regular line. Any merchandise they have is irregular or last season's goods. The labels are removed or cut to show that they're not current or regulars. One more point, we have a big successful operation, but like all manufacturers we always own goods that must be sold, that are leftovers or less than perfect. They are job lots, the kind most of our buyers can't use. This merchandise represents a lot of stock that must be liquidated. We can't sell it out of the country, we don't want to hurt loyal customers, and it represents too much money to sell for waste—to rag men."

"What you don't realize," Ben continued, "is that The Mart has given us an open order. Anytime we have $10,000 worth of goods, we ship without notice. The price is cheap but gives us a pipeline to dispose of unwanted goods. Frankly, this arrangement is as important as any we have that sells at regular retail levels. I'm sure you understand the circumstances. We want to keep our relationships pleasant and profitable, but this is one situation that we can't change, except to make sure all labels are removed in the future."

"Ben," Carol replied, "what you say, I guess, makes sense. But our policy is not to stock goods from manufacturers represented in discount stores, with or without labels, different styles, close-outs, or whatever. The problem is bigger than the department, it's one that I must take to my boss. I'll be in touch with you shortly. My boss is in Europe and I don't want to go to the general merchandise manager. He is apt to be too tough and stick to the book. All I hope is that he doesn't see the Comparison Office report and that no more complaints come in."

Carol is waiting and worried. The records show that she is doing 15% of her department volume with KICKS, a key resource that probably cannot be replaced. Even worse, the store has built up a trade for the label and competition would love for her to give up the line. They could have a party.

Rules are rules. Policy must be followed. However, sometimes rules are bent to fit circumstances.

Analyze the situation for Carol Baker, who will see her boss tomorrow following his return from Europe.

FASHION BUYING PRACTICES AND TECHNIQUES

THE APPROACH

Up to now, the discussion of merchandising has been confined to planning. Now it is time to put it into practice by using it as a tool for purchasing, the second activity of merchandising.

The following has been planned:

1. An OTB has been established.
2. Coverage for classification has been detailed:
   A. The amount for each classification.
   B. A breakdown of units for price levels within classifications.
3. A target date for stock peaking has been selected by management and the buyer will follow through by practicing the next merchandising step—buying.

WHEN TO BUY

The main reason for a market trip is to purchase merchandise. When and how often a buyer visits the market depends largely upon the:

1. Number of fashion seasons the store observes.
2. Type of store and the customer to whom it caters
3. Location of the store.
4. Rate of sale (the need for more merchandise).
5. Conditions of the market.

6. Policies of the store.
7. Condition of the economy.

TYPES OF ORDERS

Every order placed must fill a requirement. Hence, there are different types of orders for different merchandising needs.

Following is a list of the types of orders and the purposes they serve:

1. *Stock or Regular Order*—Used for stock requirements with full specifications of style numbers, quantities, delivery, sizes, and colors.
2. *Reorder*—An additional order based on successful selling.
3. *Special Order*—Placed to satisfy an individual customer request.
4. *Advance Order*—A commitment for long-term delivery, necessitated by:
   A. The nature of the goods (men's suits or quality ladies' knitwear).
   B. Specification merchandise.
   C. Special promotional merchandise.
   D. Foreign goods.
5. *Blanket Order*—One that does not have detailing for delivery. It is really a promise to place detailed orders on specified dates.
6. *Promotional Order*—A quality commitment to fulfill a planned promotional event.
7. *Open Order*—One that allows discretion to a resident buyer or manufacturer. It is given to accelerate delivery or ensure delivery of merchandise type selling well.
8. *Special Purpose Order*—A commitment for a special event.
9. *Back Order*—Outstanding commitments, in full or part, that will be completed by manufacturers.

THE MARKET TRIP FOR A NEW SEASON

PREPARATION

The buyer is concerned with culling merchandise that represents the best offering of the new season to build a desirable stock composition—one that will have favorable consumer response and therefore, result in merchandising activities as planned.

These are typical steps taken before the buyer departs for the market:

1. Arrange transportation and accommodation expenses (store paid).
2. Arrange to depart on a Sunday to make the week (or first week) most productive.
3. Advise the resident buyer of arrival time (in office).
4. Advise important manufacturers so dates can be set up, especially during peak market weeks (e.g., second week of June).

THE FIRST DAY (MONDAY)

1. Register at the resident buying office (8:30 A.M. to 9:00 A.M.).
2. Meet with resident buyer to discuss:
   A. General market outlook.
   B. Trends.
   C. Resource developments.
   D. Important information that a market specialist has digested.
   E. Review samples culled by the RBO.
   F. Obtain resident buyers' list which, in their opinion, represent the most important resources, style numbers, colors, and fabrics for the new season.

This session with the resident buyer could last one or two hours depending upon office traffic (other buyers). In some instances, two or more store buyers could work together with the office representative.

The next step varies and could be one or a combination of the following:

1. See market salesperson in the resident buying office.
2. Speak to the RBO fashion coordinator and/or divisional merchandise manager.
3. Visit stores for an orientation of current developments.
4. Begin showroom visits (market coverage).

MARKET COVERAGE TECHNIQUES

The order of visits to manufacturers is a matter of individual buyer preference. Some buyers prefer shopping an entire classification, while others may select top house of various classifications to obtain a broad point of view of fashion trends. Whatever the method, the following must be determined:

1. Direction of fashion and degree of market strength.
2. Resources that best represent fashion trends.
3. Specific styles that are representative of store needs.
4. Assurance of delivery to accommodate planned needs.

Adequate market coverage demands that a schedule should be followed that will permit the buyer to make sufficient showroom stops to:

1. See a sufficiently wide variety of merchandise.
2. Compare offerings.
3. Insure appropriateness of styles.
4. Take notes for a culling process.

Most buyers arrive in the market with a "shopping list" that is sometimes modified after consultation with the resident buyer. The list is in units of one, each representing a day. How many resources can be seen in one day is dependent upon the season and the importance of the lines being reviewed. In June, for example, the buyer can average ten to twelve stops a day; during trips at other times of the year when there is less market traffic, the stops can be more numerous. Another consideration is that orders placed earlier in regional markets or on the road (order placed with salesperson in the store) can cut down the number of vendors to be seen.

The shopping list is arranged in some order of importance to the buyer. The seasoned buyer knows that:

1. The higher priced houses reflect the important trends of the season and should be reviewed first.
2. The lowest priced houses offer "knock offs" and show the in-stock competition during the early part of the season. Therefore, they are shopped secondarily.
3. The medium priced resources are shopped later because that is where the major investments will be made.

Note: The terms higher, lowest, and medium priced resources refer to manufacturers within the range of the department's price structure. Important classifications have three price zones: low, medium, and high.

By following this pattern, the buyer is able to:

1. See the trends.
2. Compare style and values of the three sections of the buyer's market.
3. Place an order with reasonable assurance that purchases are in trend and competitively priced.

THE CULLING PROCESS (ORDER PLACEMENT)

During each showroom stop, the buyer evaluates the manufacturer's collection or styles (collection is often referred to as the line of a better priced house). The buyer can write an order after the review or make notations on a showroom pad. The procedure is dependent upon the:

1. Relationship between store and vendor (e.g., key resource).
2. Policy of the store (all orders to be confirmed by the divisional merchandise manager).
3. Need for buyer comparison (with other lines).
4. Time of visit and stock requirements.

More often, the buyer will retain the "paper," sometimes placing an informal order for later confirmation. This procedure can direct the manufacturer to pack the merchandise and wait for the store confirmation, which is the formal, or effective, order that permits shipping.

The buyer will collect showroom orders with notations of styles worthy of consideration for purchase. On each copy, the buyer has made notations that evaluate the merit of each style or group of styles. The notation system is a personal one: some use checks, double checks, triple checks; some use stars; and others use comparative words. Experience and practice results in some system most comfortable and memorable to the user. In fact, a good memory can delineate "the chaff from the wheat" without any system other than the showroom paper. It is not uncommon, too, for manufacturers to furnish a listing of all the styles offered, which permits the viewer to save time by eliminating the need for descriptions.

The buyer analyzes the orders temporarily selected, compares them against the plan to assure proper coverage of classifications, price lines, units, dollars, and any other requirements (colors, sizes, etc.).

The orders culled for placement are now set. If orders must be confirmed, they are submitted to the divisional merchandise manager, who signs them. A secretary mails them to the resource and the orders become "on order" of the department.

OTHER MARKET TRIPS

A market trip can be for one, or several of the following reasons:

1. Stock fill ins
2. Promotional merchandise
3. New market developments
4. Re-usage of money (cancellation of "dead" orders, or balances due)
5. Shopping of stores in market
6. Museum trip for fashion relevancy
7. Visit to trade associations—Wool Bureau, Cotton Council
8. New resource development
9. Steering committee activity
10. Development of advertising budget with sources of cooperative promotional money

SPECIALIZED BUYING ARRANGEMENTS

Although manufacturers show lines at established wholesale prices and the buyer does not challenge them (regular goods), there are conditions when the buyer can negotiate and receive advantages that represent an improved profit.

SALES GUARANTEE

A manufacturer offer that limits the store's liability for merchandise, the return of unsold goods. This arrangement is spelled out on the face of the order. It is not a desirable way to sell goods and is used as a strength for a "weak" manufacturer. It can also be in the form of a consignment or memorandum. The meaning of the three terms may be the same; it is dependent upon the details of the transaction.

JOB LOTS

Job lots are an assortment of goods that the manufacturer offers at reduced prices because of the inability to sell the goods in the regular way. There are many pitfalls with this type of transaction.

SPECIAL PROMOTION BUYING

The purchase of goods for less than the original cost to support a promotional event. The need for this type of merchandise for price maintaining stores is normally well after the season is underway, or at the close of a season.

PRIVATE LABEL BUYING

Some stores develop their own merchandise to obtain a combination of advantages for customer patronage and profit. Since it is exclusive merchandise, the cost is negotiated with the manufacturer. This practice is often referred to as *Specification Merchandising.*

PROCUREMENT OF ADVANTAGEOUS TERMS

A buyer for a large store understands and can use the power of placing large orders that might enhance the profit of the department. Following are possible advantages that the buyer can secure from buying power.

COST

Any reduction in cost, obviously, will bring added profit, which is the difference between the selling price and the cost. Cost reduction can be effected by:

1. *Cash Discounts*—prompt payment of bills, or through special arrangement with the vendor.
2. *Transportation Charges*—arrangement for reduction or requirement of delivery on the basis of F.O.B. store.
3. *Anticipation*—obtaining an additional discount by paying a bill before the due date (charging the manufacturer for the use of money).

DELIVERY

Timely delivery of consumer-wanted goods, either against the original order or reorder, is a merchandising advantage that presents profit-making opportunities.

EXCLUSIVITY

The ability to take merchandise out of competition makes for a variety of advantages. With buying power, it may be obtained by:

1. Exclusive right of the line in a trading area.
2. Exclusive right to a style of part of a line.
3. Earliest delivery, or sole distributorship for part of a season.
4. Developing special merchandise—private label or specification merchandise.

THE ORDER

The order is a contract which specifies responsibilities for both parties—the seller and the buyer. It is therefore encumbent upon the buyer to spell out all the arrangements in specific terms.

The order form is furnished by the store and contains terms such as warranties and conditions of sale, transportation instructions, insurance information, delivery location, and other pertinent information provided by management.

The buyer must make sure the following is detailed:

1. Beginning delivery and completion dates
2. Style numbers
3. Quantities and colors
4. Means of transportation if there is a variation from the order form general instructions.
5. Insurance terms that vary from instructions spelled out on order form.
6. Cost per style (trade practice can be cost in dozens in some popular-priced categories).
7. Special terms

Original order forms are given to the manufacturer. Duplicates are needed for the Receiving and Accounting Departments, and a third copy for the buyer to use to determine:

1. Outstanding orders
2. Receipt of goods in the department
3. Follow-up
4. Unit control records (particularly if maintained by the department

BUYER/SELLER RELATIONSHIP

The competitive nature of fashion merchandising avails opportunities for rewards that are less than honest, and the weak sometimes succumb to temptation. Both manufacturers and buyers are faced with opportunities to take advantage of temporary rewards.

A buyer is an important person in the world of fashion merchandising; trusted with considerable control over budgets for the placement of orders for merchandise. It is easy to be swayed to a position of self-importance. A level-headed person realizes the obligations of trust and maintains open relationships with all personal contacts. This leads to:

1. Personal esteem
2. Market esteem
3. Professional growth and objectivity

Case 40
Buying Ethics

Roslyn Peters is the buyer of junior coats and raincoats for a nationally known New York department store. She is a graduate of a well-known fashion college and from a six month training course as well as being an assistant buyer for three years.

Her first week in her present position was a great strain. She had never realized the weight of buying responsibilities, but after six months she started to feel comfortable. She realized that she achieved a long time hope, and now that the plateau had been reached, she had all the requisites for the job.

Her growing confidence developed to a point where she is giving advice freely to manufacturers on styling, fit, colors, and delivery.

During a visit to a stock raincoat resource, she was impressed with a style on the line.

"Look," she addressed one of the owners, "if Style 711 were available in pink, nile green, light tan, and white, it might make a great number to include in our spring catalogue."

Sam, the salesperson, responded, "With a good order, we can make it in any color you want. The fabric can be dyed to any shade. Here is Steven's color chart that, by luck, lists all the colors you mentioned. We didn't plan on them for our line, but we could be wrong."

"I'll tell you what," she said. "You check the delivery dates for the goods and final delivery to us, and I'll make sure about the space I have in the catalogue. I'll be back next week."

The following week Roslyn reported that the catalogue would feature a raincoat of her selection, in this case Style 711. The catalogue need would require a minimum of fifteen hundred garments: pink, two hundred and fifty pieces; nile green, three hundred pieces; tan, seven hundred pieces; white, two hundred pieces. Complete delivery no later than February 25.

"Great!" Sam replied. "Fill in an order and we'll get going on meeting your specifications."

"Well," Roslyn said, "I'm not really in an open-to-buy position at this time, so let me give you some specifics on your showroom pad to help you."

Roslyn did not detail department, delivery dates, or sizes. She did write in the store name and the quantities for each color.

This transaction took place the first week of October. Roslyn was pleased that she had a direction for her raincoat requirement for an important store promotion.

About two weeks later, another resource contacted Roslyn to show their new spring line. She waited until Wednesday, at which time she worked with her favorite salesperson, Dick Acker.

After the review, Dick said, "Roz, I want to show you something special. No one has seen this yet, but you're a friend."

He proceeded to show her one of the best looking styles she had seen that season.

She was smitten with it, and said, "Can I get it for February 25, complete?"

No problem she was told. The firm wanted a promotion to get it started in the New York area.

"Great, put me down for fifteen hundred pieces, and I'll confirm the order next week."

Roslyn confirmed the order and was finally set for the catalogue knowing she had a winner.

Her conscience, however, began to bother her. True, the first resource did not have a confirmed order; in fact, they did not have a formal order. But the house is used on a regular basis and she could make it up to them.

Three weeks after the negotiations had ended with the first resource, she called Sam and told him. "Circumstances have caused a change of plans. The deal is off."

"Ms. Peters, you wanted special colors which we had to buy. The quantity we laid down even includes anticipated reorder quantities. We were able to swing fast delivery because we pressured a house we do a lot of business with. You can't back out now."

"Take it easy," she answered. "We do business with you, it will be made up. Put the colors on your line and they'll sell. I'll come in and buy a few myself."

She did buy fifty coats for the season, a few in the colors discussed. This sufficed for the time being, not that Sam did not have some choice remarks for the situation that he related to his associates.

At the end of February, the catalogue was mailed to the store's customers. Sam, as a store customer, received a copy and "hit the ceiling."

"That #$%¢&* buyer, I'll fix her," was his reaction.

Sam has been around the market for many years and has a wide acquaintanceship, which included Roslyn's boss, who he knew as assistant buyer.

Sam's conversation with Roslyn's divisional merchandise manager went something like this: "Alfred, your raincoat buyer is a nervy kid who doesn't understand this business. Mark my words, she's going to hurt the store's image."

"Sam, do you mean Roslyn Peters?"

"I sure do."

Sam outlined what had taken place and summed up the conversation, "Al, we received a bona fide order from your buyer, we made commitments against it and we're stuck to the tune of $7,500. What are you going to do about it?"

The divisional manager assured Sam that he would get back to him after ferreting out the facts.

How do you feel Roslyn Peters handled herself? Is she legally correct? Was she under moral obligation? How do you think her merchandise manager handled the situation?

Case 41
Inventory Maneuvers

The average ready-to-wear manufacturer seeks the patronage of giant department stores in the largest cities of the country. Two important advantages are the quantity possibilities and the importance of the huge stores as an influence on other retailers in the trading areas.

Buyers are aware of their power and sometimes use it for some merchandising advantage. The most common is the pressure for faster than deserved delivery.

Joan Reilly, the sportswear buyer of Cook and Paley, Washington, D.C., is not only aware of the power of her position, but of every trick in the book.

On January 4, she called one of her prime resources, Dainty House, an old-line shirt manufacturer. She spoke to a principal of the company, David Isaacs, and told him of her predicament.

Her stock was very high and her merchandise manager had suggested packing some goods, returning them to the manufacturers about mid-January thus reducing the inventory for inventory taking, and in the beginning of February, buying the merchandise back intact from the manufacturer. No one gets hurt, and the department emerges looking good.

David was reluctant. He is well versed in Joan's tricks and does not like shenanigans; he is too straight-laced for merchandising gimmicks. But she is an old customer, a big user and he will not be required to open the cartons (about $10,000 at cost).

He was convinced. He agreed to accept the shipment and hold it for a week. He would relabel the cartons and rebill at original cost.

In a matter of days, the shipment was received. Large and inconvenient for Dave to store in the limited space of his New York shipping room. Joan visited the showroom and thanked Dave for his cooperation. She told him to wait for an order which she would send in a week.

"Don't send the merchandise without an order because the store will refuse the shipment, and things could get messy."

David waited one week, no order. Two weeks, and still no order. On the third week, he called the store and could not get Joan. He left a message with her assistant. It was apparent to David that she was avoiding him. Now he was worried. The merchandise was seasonal and it would be risky to hold it any longer.

On February 25, he instructed his Shipping Department to open the cartons, credit the merchandise to the store, and ship it against orders on hand. He was able to just about ship all the merchandise to stores against original orders and some reorders.

Thank goodness, he thought, my spring inventory is now down and should be in great shape in a week or two when my concentration is on spring into summer styles.

On February 28, at 9:30 A.M., Joan called long distance. "David, I placed an order in the file for the entire shipment, a copy is on the way to you. Ship it out today."

Then David related his story.

The abuse that Joan heaped on him cannot be printed. She finalized her comments, "Manufacturers are opportunistic and do not respect relationships."

This act, she claimed, was going to hurt her business because the stock will have a big hole that will take a special market trip to fill. She has been loyal, somewhat tardy on occasions, but always a person who respects obligations. The latter is the truth; Joan is tricky, but honest.

Since that day, Joan has not stepped into David's showroom. He certainly did not want to lose her business, and he did not like Joan's evaluations. One entire season went by. Finally, after continuously reading the "Buyer Arrivals," David found what he was looking for—Joan's divisional merchandise manager was in the market.

He called and met with him.

The divisional manager was sympathetic but stated: "Joan's the buyer and selector of resources. Besides she'd raise a stink if I got involved. This is her show. I'm going to do you a good turn and not mention our meeting. I'd suggest you visit her at the store and have it out."

You are David Isaac's associate. Analyze the situation and give him your best advise.

Case 42
The "Knock Off"

Gold and Silver Inc. has the best current financial retail record in the United States. Its profits on sales and returns on capital investments outstrip any larger retail organization in the country. This enviable record is the result of careful planning and imaginative follow-through by management and staff.

One of the merchandising policies is to establish in-depth stock of the most wanted items, promote on a consistent basis, and extend the selling period as long as possible.

In line with this tactic, Jeanette Jildor, the men's furnishings buyer, latched onto a shirt with a crested pocket. The sales during the season were short of phenomenal, three thousand a week, with no abatement. It just kept rolling along, to the delight of Jeanette, her merchandise manager, management, and the manufacturer, a branded resource (highly respected and a key resource to Gold and Silver).

The success of the shirt came about because of Jeanette's ingenuity. When she shopped the line, she spied a shirt that was not being pushed by the salesperson. She saw the volume potential of the shirt with the crest pocket that would be associated with blazers. Her curiosity was sufficiently aroused to address herself to the resource to ensure the following: the quality of the fabric and workmanship, the color fastness of the emblem, and the delivery support for a large scale operation.

All the factors added up favorably. Oddly enough, most buyers either sampled or did not buy the style. The road was clear to catch competitors asleep at the switch. To safeguard her position, she had secured a promise from the resource that no merchandise would be shipped in quantities to support a promotion within her trading area for two months.

She advertised—and was on target—the style took off. Week after week there was an ad that invited mail and telephone orders; the latter supported by an open switchboard on Sundays. She "milked" the item through every means possible.

The resource was most cooperative. They put aside production orders for other styles to help Jeanette, and Gold and Silver, fill their promotional needs.

After three months of record shattering sales, Jeanette decided that the "party" would probably end in two or three weeks.

She visited the resource, talked to the decision makers, and advised: "You've made my season, which will be over soon. But, have you considered the volume potential if we shave the retail price from $20.00 to $12.50, a level that will open up a new customer group; develop individual multiple sales; and above all, extend the selling season?"

"No," they stated, "you've had a ball, now it's our turn. We're going to make it a basic shirt and get the distribution we missed on the first selling round. You showed us the way, now we want to capitalize on an item that can have a run for several years."

"Be realistic," Jeanette responded, "sure your name is nationally known, but don't you know that the style is going to be "knocked off" at lower prices?"

They replied, "Apparently, you're not aware that one of the largest men's brand houses features a shirt that has been at one price for twenty years, despite 'knock offs.' "

The conversation ended with no conclusions drawn.

A day or two later, Jeanette took the shirt to a regularly used resource.

After close inspection, the production manager, in front of his boss, said, "We can make this style to cost $6.75, or even less, depending on what you want to take out."

Jeanette took a position. She placed an order in promotional depth at $6.75 in a narrow range of colors suitable for the time of year, and indicated that she would send a confirming order countersigned by her merchandise manager.

Three weeks later she advertised the shirt. The stock consisted of the original shirt marked down to $12 and the new merchandise received five days previously.

And again, she was right, the momentum continued at peak levels. Her real problem was how long this could continue and what quantity should be prepared.

The national brand house, watching events at Gold and Silver, resented the store's course of action and made their feelings known.

A letter was received by Jeanette's divisional merchandise manager which stated, "We have decided to terminate our arrangements with you and are taking steps to sell additional stores in your area, those retailers from whom we previously declined to sell."

What is your evaluation of this situation?

Case 43
Buying Practices

The Fashion Plate of Cedar Rapids, Iowa, a specialty store in the one million dollar volume class, has been shopping for a new resident buying office. They are interested in representatives that concentrate heavily on medium- to better-priced merchandise.

Manufacturers friendly to the store seem to favor Reliable Buying Office, an organization headed by a former department store merchandise manager. From all the information gathered, it would seem that Reliable Buying is the type of representative that could serve The Fashion Plate best.

There is one disturbing note that causes the store owners to hesitate. Comments, directly or indirectly, from manufacturers indicate that the Reliable Buying Office's buyers may be on the "take."

Selman, The Fashion Plate owner, visited an old and valued friend in the market, Larry Cogan, a dress manufacturer. He solicited Cogan's advice a second time and asked that no holds be barred.

"Here's the story," Cogan explained. "The resident buying business is extremely competitive and it's difficult to pay high salaries to competent personnel just from clients' fees. Extra income must be obtained by some offices from other sources. In the case of Reliable Buying, they arrange for ad mats, store catalogues, and manufacturer bulletins, all paid by manufacturers, which adds considerable office income. The buyers receive a commission on this income. It kills two birds with one stone."

"Doesn't this practice favor only cooperative manufacturers and bar the ones who refuse the office's services?"

"Not necessarily. Smart buyers know that the office's reputation is at stake, and although they are under pressure to produce income, they work with the best resources. In the long run, most good manufacturers need the services as a communication link with stores."

Selman is not convinced. The temptation to make money he feels is too much for most buyers. The selection of resources by the resident buying office must be affected by the opportunity to make money. This is the only factor that bothers him in his decision to have Reliable Buying represent him. He is so concerned and confused that he inquires at top houses in several different merchandise classifications. The information is the same, not one resource gave Reliable Buying Office a rating less than excellent.

He finally took the bull by the horns and made a date to see Reliable Buying. His plans include stating his feelings about the office practice of sharing its income with resident representatives.

How do you think the Reliable Buying Office president is going to rebut Selman's unhappiness and prove that his office offers the best resources despite buyer involvement in selling an office service to manufacturers.

Case 44
The Off-Price
Promotion

Howard Peterson, the basement dress buyer for Perkins Department Store, was meeting with Paul Jacobs, the basement ready-to-wear merchandise manager, a weekly event. Perkins is a large, promotional department store located in New York City. Although there are six suburban branch stores, only the New York City store has a basement operation.

This meeting took place at the beginning of the month and Jacobs, while reviewing the department's figures, remarked to Peterson, "Say, Howard, you have to come up with a big promotion to meet and hopefully beat your figures for the last week of this month. Last year you were lucky and latched on to an item that was in trend and you rode it to make these tremendous figures. I don't see any strong trends in sight at this time, so you better go out and hold a gun to a manufacturer you do a big business with. . . ."

Howard replied glumly: "You're right, chief, there's nothing hot in sight. And to tell you the truth, I've been worrying about those figures for a while now. My key resources do not seem to be in a position to dump a large amount of goods. I'm really up a tree. . . ."

His merchandise maanger came to his rescue.

"Tell you what—the way I figure it, you need to get three thousand units to sell for about $10 each to make your figures. To meet your last year's record, you should pay about $5.75, no more. I'll get you about $30,000 in open-to-buy for the event and also arrange for extra advertising money for a full-page ad in two papers. That ought to do the trick, but, Howard, you better get some good merchandise at a price . . . the ads have to generate a sellout for us if we're to come out all right."

Howard Peterson went into the market and found a dress manufacturer, who had been after him for a long time and who was very eager to get his foot into Perkins' door. Howard had made several unimportant purchases from Goodman Frocks and he had found their dresses to be nicely made. Sensing that this was his big chance to become a key resource with Perkins, Sy Goodman went all-out in shaving his prices and insuring delivery well in advance of the promotion.

Shortly after this, Paul Jacobs called Howard and told him that a small problem had arisen. "Howard, I'm ashamed to tell you that the general merchandise manager was not able to come across with the whole $4,000 we need for the ads. We can't cut the ads—we need all the ad space we can buy to make the ad scream *PRICE*. I was only able to get half the ad money, we'll need $2,000 to pay for the rest."

Peterson was incredulous because the inference was unmistakable. Jacobs wanted him to get a $2,000 co-op ad contribution on a close-out and he knew that was almost impossible. However, he dutifully went to Sy Goodman and asked him for the money to pay for the ad. Goodman looked at him as if he were mad; he swore a holy oath that he was losing money on each of the three thousand dresses that he had sold to Perkins. He pointed out what Howard already knew, that he was taking this deal only because he was hoping to do business later with Perkins on a more profitable basis.

Howard reported back to Jacobs and informed him of his inability to get the ad money.

"There is only one way out," Paul Jacobs replied. "We'll have to load the invoice. Instead of $5.75 we'll ask Goodman Frocks to bill us at $6.50 per dress; and then we'll retail them for $11.00 instead of the $10.00 we originally planned. Also, ask Goodman to throw in some dresses that can genuinely be sold at retail for $25.00 so that we can legitimately advertise '*VALUES UP TO $25.00 FOR $11.00.*' We'll then charge the manufacturer back $0.75 for each garment to cover the $2,000 that we need for the ad money. In the final analysis, we'll get the volume and sacrifice some markup."

And so it went. The merchandise arrived at the store in time and it was ticketed at $11. The ad was to appear on Wednesday evening for the big Thursday to Saturday selling period.

After dinner on Wednesday evening, Howard Peterson went to buy the morning paper. He found his full-page ad and was quite pleased with the way it looked. But to his horror, he discovered that on the page following his big promotion there was one from Sommers Department Store, their chief competitor. The Sommers' ad appeared to feature the identical merchandise, but the dresses were priced at $9.95 each. Both ads had photographs illustrating what appeared to be very similar merchandise.

Howard ran to the phone and called his merchandise manager at home exclaiming, "Paul, we've been killed—did you see the ads?"

Jacobs replied, "Howard, *you* selected the merchandise. Who told you to buy from a thief?"

The next morning Howard Peterson stopped at Sommers Department Store on the way to work and looked at the merchandise on sale. Of course, it was the same—style numbers, colors, sizes, etc.

No customer in her right mind could fail to see that it was the same merchandise at a dollar lower than it was at Perkins across the street. It is well known in the trade that the basement dress customer is a very smart shopper.

When Howard arrived at his desk, there was the expected message to see Jacobs at once. Jacobs went right to work on Howard.

"You as a seasoned buyer should have known how to select a resource and how to buy an off-price promotion."

If you were Howard Peterson, how would you reply to this criticism and how would you propose to get out of this situation?

Case 45
Mort Heller Made a Big Boo-Boo

It was almost 5:30 P.M. on Friday when Mort Heller entered the deserted showroom of PANTS OF AMERICA, INC. All the personnel had rushed out before 5:30 P.M. and only Art Blatt, one of the owners of the firm, was still puttering around. He was meeting his wife at 6:30 P.M. at a nearby midtown restaurant for dinner, prior to attending the ballet that evening. Blatt did not anticipate much enjoyment that evening because he did not quite share his wife's enthusiasm for the ballet.

Thus, Art Blatt was quite surprised to see anyone coming into the showroom at that late hour, especially on a Friday and especially, Mort Heller. He had known Mort Heller, one of the top buyers in the popular-priced sportswear field and regarded as a wheeler-dealer of great renown, for a long time.

Mort Heller was the head sportswear buyer for Small's, one of New York City's (and probably the country's) biggest fashion discount operators. Small's had been in the underselling aspect of fashion merchandising long before the discount house as we know it today had been born. And Mort Heller had grown up in this business and was one of its shrewdest and most respected practitioners.

After effusive greetings were exchanged, Art Blatt inquired as to Heller's presence in his showroom at that late hour.

"Art, you've got to help me out," replied Mort Heller. "I need to line up a big promotion before I leave for Korea and Taiwan on Sunday. I'll be away for almost a month and I have some big figures to make during that time. I've plenty of goods on hand or coming in but I need at least one more big promotion to keep the pot boiling. Art, what have you got for me?"

Art Blatt shook his head. "Mort, it's 5:30 P.M. on a Friday night, the end of a hard week. Go home, or better still, come downstairs with me and I'll buy you a drink. You know our merchandise is not for you. Our quality is too high and our prices are not on your level. Forget the whole idea."*

True to form, Mort Heller persisted in his efforts to have Art

---

* Of course, this is only the first of several ploys that both men will engage in during this encounter. This one is designed by our pants manufacturer to whet the buyer's appetite.

Blatt show him some "red hot bargains." Mort was weaned on the theory that all manufacturers have merchandise to dispose of—his job was to pry it loose before someone else did.

For his part, Art Blatt continued to insist that his merchandise was too good for Small's.*

Art Blatt believes that he is in a particularly fortunate position at this moment. He knows that a big wheel such as Small's Mort Heller would not be in his showroom on a Friday evening after 5:30 P.M. unless he needed goods badly. It is also probably true that Mort has been out all day looking for promotional goods and he has evidently failed to come up with a successful promotion. Hence this last-ditch attempt.

Playing his hand carefully, Art Blatt appears ready to give in, and grudgingly admits that maybe he might find something for Mort. This is the moment Mort has been waiting for and he demands to see the inventory sheets. This is a discount buyer's regular off-price promotion ploy because from those sheets he can readily see the stock condition (in sizes, colors, etc.) of each number. From these sheets, the buyer can determine the weak spots in the manufacturer's inventory and can exploit these weaknesses in order to drive the price down further.

But PANTS OF AMERICA, INC. as well as many of their contemporaries are well prepared for these moments when discount buyers are driving for lowest prices possible on the best goods available. Art Blatt's office people have actually prepared three separate inventory sheets and only when they are added together is the true inventory picture visible. Art gives Mort one of these sheets which indicates only one-third of the stock involved. Mort Heller, after studying the sheet and checking the style numbers, finally decides to settle on a group of slacks that are priced at $12.75 and $14.75 wholesale. In the ensuing bargaining, Art Blatt offers them to Mort at a flat price of $9.75 each. Mort Heller counters with an offer to take all he has in stock at $3.75 each. In the final agreement Mort buys the entire stock at $5.50 a pair, net. (Remember, in his own mind, Art Blatt was prepared to go as low as $4 each.) "Mort, you have the deal on your terms," said the manufacturer. "But I still feel that you should not buy the pants. Our merchandise is too good for your customers. You're going to mark them $8.50 or $8.95, but your regular custom-

---

* Actually, PANTS OF AMERICA, INC. is loaded with goods for off-price promotions. But it would not do for the manufacturer to seem anxious to sell because that would automatically drive the price down. In fact, Art Blatt had a big lot of pants that normally sold at $12.75 wholesale that he was ready to unload for as low at $4.00 per pair.

ers look for this kind of merchandise at a top of $7.50, and that's garbage. So, why bother—I'm cutting out my label and your customers don't recognize good merchandise. They only think of price."

"Don't downgrade my customers. They know and appreciate good value and workmanship," replied the discounter.

"Well, Mort, this is my final advice. You're buying 6,000 pair of pants, a $33,000 order at cost. And you're buying them against my better judgment. I'll have them in your receiving room early next week. And after that, you own them. We don't sell merchandise at these prices with rubber bands attached. We don't take anything back on a close-out like this. Don't come crying to me about your mortgage on the house in Great Neck or your kids' orthodontist bills. You own the goods and if they don't sell, you'll eat them. Do me one last favor—don't buy the pants—let me close up and let's have a drink."

"Listen, Art," Heller said, "who do you think you're talking to? I buy more merchandise this way in one month than you sell in a year."

Art Blatt tried once more in the elevator to dissuade Mort Heller from buying the pants. He warned him again of the *no return policy*. But the deal was final. Mort Heller left for the Orient on Sunday as scheduled.

A month later, Heller returned to the PANTS OF AMERICA showroom. The door opened and Mort crawled in on his hands and knees.

The receptionist grabbed the nearest phone and screamed, "Mr. Blatt, come quickly. There's a crazy man crawling around the showroom floor licking my shoes."

You guessed it, dear reader, the pants promotion was one big flop. Mort Heller was using the final ploy to mitigate his potential loss, getting on his hands and knees and begging for relief.

Art Blatt, of course, remained adamant and refused to take back any of the merchandise, give Mort any co-op ad money, or make any other concessions on the basis that professionalism includes the ability to own up to mistakes, particularly when the deal is on a no return basis.

What advice can you give Mort Heller? Better still, can you tell him what he failed to do or what he overlooked?

XV

SALES PROMOTION

DEFINITION

Sales promotion is the third "P" of merchandising; it follows planning and purchasing, and should lead to the last "P"—profit. Profit can only be realized as a result of selling, therefore all retailers are deeply concerned with the sales promotion effort.

The term, sales promotion, has been defined in numerous ways, but for our purpose, it is any means that influences the purchase of fashion apparel. From the buyer's point of view, the two major objectives are:

1. Customer patronage for the department
2. Acceleration of sales

Naturally, a store requires the buyer to plan for and participate in events that have wider objectives: store patronage motives, institutional values, and prestige.

What strategies and tactics are used are dependent upon what customer group is sought. Lord and Taylor and Korvette's, for example, employ different techniques to influence their selected audiences.

FASHION PROMOTION MEDIA
(including personal selling)

The following means of promotion are used to influence customer buying decisions.

PERSONAL SELLING

Personal selling ranges from full- to no-service. The level of availability is dependent upon the nature of the retail operation. Unfortunately, even where it is available, the quality is often less than adequate. Since it is the highest cost of doing business outside of the cost of the merchandise, it is reasonable to assume that it will deteriorate even further. Good salesmanship can avail all or any combination of the following advantages:

1. Highlighting garment features
2. Motivating customers to purchase apparel
3. Enhancing patronage motives for the department
4. Solving customers' "problems"
5. Suggesting additional merchandise
6. Obtaining customer feedback

NEWSPAPERS

Newspapers, as a medium, receive the lion share of a fashion department's promotional budgets because:

1. They reach 90% of all U.S. families with an appeal to each member of the family.
2. The cost per reader is less costly than any other means.
3. They have the longest span of potential customer interest. The consumer reads newspapers at his leisure which makes for the greatest concentration and impact.
4. The response to advertisements is relatively fast and measurable.

MAGAZINES, INDEPENDENT SHOPPING PUBLICATIONS, RADIO, TELEVISION

Magazines, independent shopping publications, radio, and television are all used in a minor way, with greatest concentration on institutional values. It should be mentioned that television can be the next best form of advertising to personal selling. It has color, motion, sound, and the human voice (spoken by a well-trained, attractive person). Television has all the elements for fashion selling, except the cost.

DIRECT MAIL

Direct mail is a widespread form of fashion merchandise promotion, most often in the form of statement enclosures and catalogues. Newspaper ads that feature mail and telephone, although not considered direct mail, are strongly related to it and represent a well-used, successful means to volume selling by many stores.

Direct mail and mail and telephone advertising are of deep concern to the buyer because:

1. They represent a big business that continues to grow.
2. Increased customer leisure time, oddly, has an influence in establishing them as a modern way of shopping.
3. Lack of stores' quality personal service has further influenced impersonal shopping habits.
4. Customer recognition that impersonal selling methods require high standards of quality and garment specifications. (Organizations that use mail and other impersonal methods.)
5. They afford the retailer the ability to reach particular groups of people (by income, ethnic value, charge customers, etc.).

FASHION SHOWS

Fashion shows are one of the most exciting methods of influencing customers to purchase fashion goods. Practically everyone enjoys the drama and excitement of a show of new fashions that include: attractive models, music, and a festive atmosphere. Fashion shows also show fashion authority, no small attribute to attract customers.

A small store is at no disadvantage and can stage periodic events to prove its importance in the fashion world of its community.

Larger stores offer presentations in auditoriums and selling departments, frequently department showings in the form of "trunk" shows featuring merchandise of the forward season, sometimes with a famous designer present.

WINDOW DISPLAYS

Window displays can be likened to the apparel one wears, they are a reflection of attitudes. Although the buyer does not control when merchandise can be featured in windows and in trafficked areas, what can be displayed on the floor is largely in the hands of the buyer. Floor displays are opportunities to expose merchandise to traffic and thereby influence customers. Wherever possible, merchandise used in other forms of promotion should be featured in the windows for added impetus and customer convenience (where to find it in the store).

It is interesting to note that many apparel chain stores in shopping centers do a minimum or no newspaper advertising, depending wholly on location and traffic to obtain a local market share of fashion business. In these instances, window displays are most carefully planned and evaluated.

FLOOR DISPLAYS

Of equal importance, perhaps greater for the buyer, is the floor display of a fashion department. This is where the store attitude, department point of view, and fashion knowledge are revealed to the customer. A smart buyer seeks, accepts, and uses the aid of all staff personnel to make the department "smart" looking and the merchandise salable. The fashion coordinator and display people are staff personnel who are available for help or in charge of the activity.

RESPONSIBILITY FOR SALES PROMOTION

Since promotion is one of the major components of the retail mix (and merchandising activities), management sets rules concerning:

1. Goals
2. Format (logo, artwork, layout, etc.)
3. Budget (percent to net sales)
4. Media
5. Responsibility
6. Calendar of events

In a larger store, sales promotion is the responsibility of the Sales Promotion Department (sometimes called the Advertising Department), with a separate sub-division which concentrates on activities involving catalogues and direct mailing pieces.

THE BUYER'S ROLE

Obviously, merchandise required to support promotional events is purchased by the buyer.

The event starts with a store plan drawn up by the general merchandise manager who then allocates budgets to the various divisions. The divisional merchandise manager then plans a calendar of events with each buyer which includes:

1. Date
2. Space
3. Purpose

The discussion additionally includes the following merchandising factors with strong buyer input:

1. The buyer's selection of resources
2. The merchandise
3. Volume potential
4. Reorder probabilities
5. Cutoff date of selling
6. Markup
7. Retail value
8. Unit requirements
9. Timing

THE PROMOTIONAL PURCHASE

The first step by the buyer is a plan to purchase merchandise against the available open-to-buy with the realization that:

1. The delivery must be made in advance of the promotion date.
2. The commitment will be against the open-to-buy for the month in which delivery is made (as stated above).
3. The required budget for the event was provided for in the Merchandise Plan.

The second step is to visit the selected resources, or seek resources suitable for the purpose.

These are some of the conditions that will have to be satisfied:

1. The appropriateness of the merchandise such as style, quality, price, color.
2. Resource relationship
   A. Key, or preferred, resources are most desirable since customer acceptance of the merchandise is already known.
   B. Delivery dependability.
3. Reorder possibilities—backup merchandise to be held by the manufacturer. In catalogue merchandising, this is a critical need. Errors of stock omission are serious miscalculations.

After all these conditions have been met, the buyer places the commitment (the order).

The final step is the follow-up. A vigilance to ensure timely delivery well in advance of the date of promotion. Non-delivery is considered a calamity for which management accepts no excuse.

THE MECHANICS OF THE PROMOTION

As discussed, every large organization has a Sales Promotion or Advertising Department which is responsible for:

1. The purchase of space (catalogue or direct mail requirements)
2. Production of the promotion
   A. Copy
   B. Layout
   C. Artwork

The buyer furnishes merchandise and information about it so that the specialists in the Promotion Department can develop the advertisement.

Once the work is finished, it is submitted to the buyer in proof form so that the buyer can verify all the details and suitability.

A BUYER CHECK LIST FOR SALES PROMOTION PURCHASES

1. Merchandise and resources should typify the store's image.
2. Promotional values should be realistic and honest. The Better Business Bureau has standards for: "regularly," "usually," "formerly," etc. Customers are not fooled by sharp practices.
3. Promotions should be supported with adequate stock. Early fall catalogue responses, for example, that necessitate letters of delayed delivery are annoying to customers.
4. Caution should dictate that a rate of sale should be established before "plunging" into merchandise for volume production.
5. Specification buyers (Sears, Wards, and Penneys) are experts in filling catalogue requirements because they:
   A. Research the makers.
   B. Visit production facilities.

    C. Submit specifications.

    D. Double-check samples for specifications and quality. Other buyers who do specification buying for promotional events should heed these practices.

6. A buyer should understand the purpose of an ad and act accordingly.

7. The immediate sales returns from a mail and telephone order may be deceptive. If the ad is too flattering to the merchandise the returns can be heavy.

8. Newspaper advertisements can be more effective if:

    A. Window and floor displays reinforce the featured merchandise.

    B. Sales personnel is properly advised and given reasons for the promotion.

9. Unsuccessful ads should not be repeated.

10. New resources should be avoided if possible: their merchandise is new to the department, the selling rate is unknown, and the quality level is not established.

11. Cooperative advertising money should be considered as an added feature of a purchase, not the reason for it.

12. The buyer's first loyalty is to the stock of the department. It should be studied for realistic assessment of current value and marked down, if conditions warrant, to levels that reflect current value.

13. The markdown of regular goods can be a bargain for customers and reinforce patronage motives.

14. Lower priced levels should not be promoted at the beginning of a season. This is the time for higher priced concentration. Customers will look for lower prices later.

15. Off-price promotions should not be purchased in the absence of a manufacturer's inventory showing styles, colors, sizes, and quantities.

16. Orders for promotion of this type should be detailed against a manufacturers inventory, e.g. *specific* quantities, styles, colors.

17. A warehouse visit to inspect the goods is an excellent practice.

18. Job lot buying is a dangerous practice. It is available because of someone's mistakes; the second mistake can be the buyer's.

19. Promotions are a partnership arrangement between the manufacturer and the store—the manufacturer should be made aware that the store's communication also affects his

relationships with customers—the store's and his own (your competition and his channels of distribution).
20. All promotional orders should specify:
   A. The fact that the order is for a promotion.
   B. The date of delivery should be discussed in depth. If there is any current problem the buyer is flirting with later trouble.
   C. All special conditions should be written on the face of the order as a confirmation of agreed terms. Conditions written on a later received confirmation order form may go unheeded.

CONCLUSION

Sales promotion is a major part of the retail marketing effort and continued strong selling results depend on effective merchandising activities. The sales promotion effort must be honest, consistent, and representative of what the store is about. Every store, naturally, has a policy of what its promotional activities include and what results are expected.

A critical standard of measurement of buyer efficiency is the selling record. Retail profit is the result of a domino effect. Good planning leads to a well balanced stock; effective promotions of well purchased merchandise adds up to profit as planned—the name of the game.

The promotional results of every purchase event are recorded and used as the experience factor for future events. Buyers usually maintain a diary in which all merchandising and correlory information are entered:

1. Sales—volume for each day
2. Weather
3. Promotional event (all details—medium, space size, merchandise, etc.)
4. Any activity that influenced the merchandising results of that day. This is further evidence that:
   A. All planning is based on experience plus anticipation.
   B. All merchandising activities are measurable.
   C. Maximum profit is the result of well-conceived plans.

Case 46
The Founder's Day
Special

The Young Company, a giant department store in Orlando, Florida, runs a storewide clearance sale every October. The event lasts for one week and features goods from stock, ranging from 25% to 40% off regular prices. The yearly event has always been highly successful and satisfactory from two points of view: (1) It helps the store to clear merchandise and brings the inventory levels down to accommodate new holiday merchandise; and (2) it yields customer satisfaction.

Every buyer submits a list of items to be included in the ad. The list describes the merchandise, the regular retail prices, and the new reduced prices. The ads are then published in the same way, in list form.

Ethel Frommer, the coat buyer, submitted her list to her divisional merchandise manager, who reviewed it for sufficient quantities, original values, and new price levels. They were satisfactory and approved.

Two days before the ad was to appear, Sidney Smith, the general merchandise manager, visited the department with a proof copy of the first series of ads.

He said, "Ethel, I'd like to review the merchandise and check it against the copy."

"Fine," replied Ethel.

Smith entered the reserve stock room off the selling floor and checked each group to get a feeling for the bargain aspect of the merchandise. As he was nearing the end of his research, he spotted one group of coats, originally $50 marked down to $25.

"Ethel, didn't you run these coats at $25 last month?"

"Yes, I did," she replied.

"And wasn't it a bust, about four coats out of seventy-five," he retorted.

"You have a fine memory, that's the case."

"Well, you aren't going to run them again. We don't repeat failures," he stated in no uncertain terms.

"Please, market conditions have changed, cold weather and a sparse market supply make these coats worth $50. In fact, if I had to fill in colors and sizes, I'd have to pay the regular price, $27.50. At

$25, the customers are getting the bargain of the season," she pleaded.

"Sorry," Smith responded. "Go up to the Advertising Department and change the price to $15. First, of course, get your markdown book and record the reduction."

"Yes sir," she replied.

Ethel is hopping mad. She feels the decision is arbitrary and without respect for her judgment.

As an objective observer, analyze the situation.

Case 47
Does No Mean Never

Helen Miles was hired as the sportswear buyer for Becker and Howell of Spokane, Washington. The store is moderate sized and except for sportswear, enjoys a reputable and successful ready-to-wear operation. A series of buyers, changes of department location, and probable misinterpretation of wanted merchandise have resulted in a sportswear operation well below the achievements of the other apparel departments.

Helen, a successful buyer for a large Chicago store, was offered an unusually large salary and bonus arrangement, which she accepted. That was six months ago.

She assessed the situation as one that would take a year or two to correct. In fact, she submitted a report to her merchandise manager which included: re-alignment of resources, development of important key resources, restructure of price lines to higher levels, a series of promotions—both product and institutional. Her divisional merchandise manager was impressed and complimented her for a well-conceived plan.

Yesterday, Helen held a meeting with her boss, during which she said, "I know that the store's policy is not to advertise classifications that have natural high consumer interest during the holiday selling period. What I have in mind is a promotional series of three ads for sweaters. The merchandise is great, the makers are familiar to me from my former job and all three will pay one hundred percent of the space cost. It's a wonderful way to get the department rolling by featuring the right merchandise, very much in demand, with character, that will show our customers a lively sportswear department."

"Great idea," he responded, "too bad our policy won't permit it. You know the rule. It was pointed out during our conversation prior to your employment."

"True," she said, "but please remember that it will cost the store nothing. Besides, I didn't really realize the poor shape of the department. It needs all the help it can get. Let's face it, rules are meant to be bent. How about putting the facts before the general merchandise manager and have him make an exception?"

Shaking his head to indicate a negative response, "No, I think we'll play the game by the rules. We can use prominent floor displays, possibly get a store front window, even use the elevator corridors for extra displays."

Helen is a live wire and doesn't accept "no" very easily. She is determined, and confidentially, she feels she is smarter than her immediate boss.

How do you think Helen Miles should proceed?

Case 48
Double Trouble

Mail-order firms are extremely careful in their development of catalogue merchandise. They use every form of insurance: the right resource, widely accepted merchandise, established standard specifications, on-target delivery dates.

Alan Kale, the ladies' coordinate buyer for J.L. Surrey, one of the largest mail-order organizations in the country, is a bright, young man who is fully cognizant of all the "rights" for the proper development of merchandise.

During the negotiations with vendors for the big fall catalogue, an executive of one of the leading chemical companies held several meetings with Kale and his merchandise manager. The executive was anxious for Surrey to introduce a new synthetic in their fall catalogue and offered a liberal sum for cooperative advertising. Alan's boss was delighted. The chemical company is a huge organization with an international reputation and a long list of successful man-made fiber introductions to the market.

The essence of the meetings was that: Surrey would have an exclusive in coordinates (sweaters and slacks) for the fall season (through September); the chemical company would underwrite delivery of yarn to any manufacturer of Kale's choice; and that it was a sure-fire success. (Surrey has "captive" spinners and can influence yarn delivery dates.)

Despite the chemical company's reputation, Alan was somewhat leery about pioneering a new yarn, but did not express these feelings to his boss.

In due course, Alan made the necessary arrangements for styles, colors, sizes, and quantities with one of his top resources. The order was given in January for May 30 delivery.

Samples were submitted by the manufacturer for specification checking. They were precise. On or about May 25, the entire shipment was made to Surrey's distribution center.

As usual, the fall catalogue was mailed during the month of June and orders for the two styles were heavy. Alan checked with the reorder clerk who was poised to place an additional order for another ten thousand outfits at $22.50 each. A great record after only two weeks. Then things began to happen. Customer returns came in droves with the explanation that the garments did not hold shape. Once they were stretched, there was no recovery to the original dimensions.

Alan was dumbfounded. He called the chemical company and they promised to get on the situation immediately and sent yarn and production experts without delay. Kale called the manufacturer who could not suggest any solution since the yarn was new to him. The manufacturer would wait for the chemical company professionals and solicit their advice.

Kale's merchandise manager was hardly solicitous. Indeed, he was rather abrupt.

"I made the introduction, obtained advertising cooperation and showed you the way to obtain a half million dollar page return. You're the merchandise expert. You selected and arranged for the styling. Our facilities were open to test the yarn. Did you work with our quality control people?"

Alan had to admit that he had not checked with quality control. He assumed that a yarn from that chemical company had to be perfect.

Surrey at this point printed letters of merchandise omission and accepted all returns without question. Alan was now charged with a stock at $225,000 at cost. He was aware that the manufacturer was not about to share in the loss (he was reluctant to work with the yarn in the first place, but agreed after he made several samples that seemed right). He did say he would not be responsible for any yarn characteristics since he had no real knowledge of its performance.

Alan has just received a memorandum from the general merchandise manager. He has the feeling that one of two things were probably going to happen. Either he will be fired or, if he is not fired, he will be severly reprimanded and would be in bad graces for as long as he stays with the firm.

If you were Alan Kale, how would you analyze the situation and make a case for yourself with the big boss.